Mozart

✻✻✻

W. A. Mozart.

Richard Baker

❊❊❊

Mozart

❊❊❊

*with 81 illustrations
and a map*

Thames and Hudson

AUTHOR'S NOTE

I would like to express my gratitude to Timothy Joss for his
far-reaching research assistance and to Margaret Dowson who
deciphered my manuscript and typed it perfectly.

❋ ❋ ❋

Filmset by Tameside Filmsetting Limited, Ashton-under-Lyne, Lancashire
Printed and bound in Great Britain by The Pitman Press, Bath
Illustrations originated and printed by BAS Printers Limited,
Over Wallop, Hampshire

Contents

Foreword

In every age, to a greater or lesser extent, the paymaster has called the piper's tune and musicians have always had to please someone if they are not to starve. Nowadays state agencies and civic authorities, benevolent trusts and commercial firms have taken over from wealthy individuals as patrons of music. Such organizations, given a glimmer of sense, can often show a remarkably tolerant face to experiment; indeed, the more avant-garde the opus, the more credit the patron will hope to gain for far-sighted disinterest.

It was not always so. Those who kept Handel and Haydn alive were not prepared to wait for posterity's judgment; they wanted to be pleased as instantly by the music as by their food and tended to judge both by much the same criteria. Novelty? Well, just a soupçon perhaps, but not too much and not too often.

Of course there were liberal patrons. But even the best of them demanded an attachment which could seem like slavery to an artist of spirit. Mozart was such an artist. He rebelled against the respectable chains his father had learned to wear. Yet for the rest of his life – such were the conditions prevailing at the time – he was searching for a steady appointment at court which would spare him the anxieties of a free-lance existence.

7

Beethoven was Mozart's junior by only fourteen years, but he belonged to a different age. The irreverence which Mozart generally confined to private letters erupted in Beethoven's open refusal to doff his hat to authority; the revolutionary spirit was abroad, and the Romantic tide was starting to flood, bringing with it the cult of the individual. Though Mozart bridled at the old system, he had to live with it, and that included working within the established musical language of the day. No furious smashing of pianofortes for him, no bursting the barriers of symphonic form with choral finales. Instead, a disciplined approach which kept the strongest emotions within the context of musical good manners. 'The passions, whether violent or not,' wrote Mozart on the subject of opera, 'should never be so expressed as to reach the point of causing disgust; and music, even in situations of the greatest horror, should never be painful to the ear but should flatter and charm it and thereby always remain music.'

To make conscious use of music as a vehicle for conveying the composer's own feelings in the fashion of Berlioz or Tchaikovsky would have been even more unthinkable in Mozart's time. There was then a European fraternity of creative musicians who drew on a common melodic tradition; no great store was set on originality and indeed one musicologist has estimated that 80 per cent of Mozart's tunes occurred also in the music of his contemporaries.* Gradually this fraternal spirit was eroded, giving way to a competitiveness which demanded marked individual styles, almost a kind of brand warfare. Composers in Mozart's day experienced none of the anguish of 'finding their own voice' which besets serious composers of the twentieth century. Such atomization

---

* B. Szabolcsi: 'Folk Music – Art Music – History of Music', *Studia Musicologica* (Budapest), vii (1965), 171–9

simply did not exist, for the composer was merely required to produce to order a certain quantity of an established commodity.

Yet for many people Mozart is the greatest of composers. No words can do justice to his simplicity or his sublimity; he is, like Shakespeare, ageless. But for all his transcendent genius, it is helpful to see him too as a child of his time. The power of Mozart was after all generated by an eighteenth-century dam.

Chapter One

The World Mozart Entered

✵✵✵

A modern visitor aware of the grace of Mozart's music may well be surprised by the solid grandeur of his native city. The great Cathedral of St Rupert, dedicated with a week of celebration in 1628, has a massive dignity not always associated with the Baroque; the towers and spires and courtyards are on a splendid scale, and the Archbishop's Palace, which occupies a large area in the centre of the old city, is fit for a monarch. Appropriately, since the Prince-Archbishops of Salzburg had exercised temporal as well as spiritual sway over the city and district since Bishop Rupert was sent there as a missionary in the year 696.

The city, like Edinburgh, is dominated by a medieval castle, the Hohensalzburg, and a hilly ridge runs from the fortress along the southern edge of the city to the Mönchsberg. In ancient days this no doubt formed an admirable defensive feature, but it also had the effect of compressing a mini-metropolis into a small space bounded on its northern flank by the River Salzach. Archbishop Wolf Dietrich, who inaugurated the building of the Cathedral and the Palace, extended the city across the river by building what is now the Mirabell Palace on the other side for his mistress; but for all its spreading growth, then and later, there is still something claustrophobic about Salzburg.

Or is that feeling merely inspired by the knowledge that Mozart was eager to leave the place?

He was born at a time when conditions were changing for the musician. His father Leopold, an able man who graduated with distinction from a Jesuit school in Augsburg and continued a good all-round education at Salzburg University before abandoning his general studies in favour of music, settled for what was still the most frequent employment for musicians – a permanent post in a noble household. He served five successive Prince-Archbishops of Salzburg for a total of forty years, never quite achieving the coveted title of Kapellmeister, Master of the Music. But his conditions of service did not prevent him publishing, in 1756, the year of his famous son's birth, a 'Violin School' which achieved an international reputation and is still studied today. Leopold was very well aware that a world existed outside Salzburg and was almost too eager that his son should succeed in it.

A number of eighteenth-century composers managed to break away from their aristocratic patrons and make their own terms with the musical public. This was partly because a new middle-class audience was growing up. Subscription concerts had begun in large cities like London, Hamburg and Paris, where the famous Concert Spirituel was established in 1725; numerous music societies were being formed, musical periodicals started to appear in the early years of the century and publishers like Haydn's Artaria were beginning to assert an influence which was to become dominant in later times.

Various opportunities, then, were presented to the musician in the mid-eighteenth century. In his early years Handel made a living as an organist in Halle, produced his first operas in Italy with the help of aristocratic patrons, and became briefly Kapellmeister to the Elector of Hanover. Then he decamped to London where he entered into contracts with theatres, continued to produce works for the stage under the auspices of the Royal Academy of Music, formed in 1719, exercised the privilege of copyright granted him by King George I in 1720 and, apart from a few bad patches, made enough money to give charity performances and become a regular subscriber to the Musicians' Benevolent Fund from its inception in 1738.

Bach, after a spell as Kapellmeister to Prince Leopold of Anhalt-Cöthen, became Cantor of St Thomas' School in Leipzig and spent the rest of his life as a city council employee. He was required to inform the Burgomaster if he wished to leave Leipzig and had to promise not to make church music 'too long or too operatic', but he was able to enhance his modest salary with various 'perks' and to extend his scope by working for the University and directing the Telemann Singing Society. This was a 'collegium musicum', another increasingly popular means of taking music outside the precincts of church and castle.

Haydn in his late twenties entered the service of the Esterházy family, becoming Kapellmeister in 1766. Though he intensely disliked the isolation of Prince Nicolaus' country estate at Esterháza, where the musicians had to spend much of their time, it was there that Haydn produced some of his finest and most inventive music. His meeting with the publisher Artaria took place in 1780, after which date his Esterházy contract allowed him to travel and to promote his compositions as he wished. 'The free arts and the beautiful art of composition', wrote Haydn in 1778, 'tolerate no shackling. The spirit and the soul must be free if one would gather one's deserts.' Haydn fortunately lived long enough to reap an appropriate reward. In 1790 he retired from service to the Esterházy family with a pension which was subsequently increased in stages, made his immensely successful journeys to London and settled in Vienna where he lived in old age, having learned how to preserve his economic independence. (But long before leaving his aristocratic patrons, they had rewarded him with marks of high esteem, none apparently more telling than Prince Esterházy's order to the wine super-intendent 'to deliver one quart of officers' wine' to Haydn daily.)

Mozart's forerunner in restoring truth and dignity to the musical stage, Christoph Willibald Gluck, married a rich woman, which has always been one way to balance a budget. He too worked for a variety of employers, from princely households to the management of the Paris Opéra. His last years brought disappointment and ill-health, but he rode out daily in his own carriage from a fine home in Vienna, where he was highly respected as a leading practitioner of the craft of music.

In the more limited community of Salzburg, Leopold Mozart, a reserved man conscious of his status and not given to indiscriminate friendship with his musical colleagues, considered himself the equal of successful merchants and other professional people. Thus he established friendly relations with, among others, the families of the Court Surgeon Andreas Gilowsky, the Chancellor Franz von Mölk, the Prince's personal physician Dr Silvester Barisani and Georg Josef Robinig, a hardware dealer and Barisani's landlord.

As an educated man whose subjects of study had included Dialectic and Physics, Leopold would have been open to the prevailing mood of 'the age of enlightenment', with its rational critique of all feudal institutions, its belief in social and political rights and in progress towards a more equitable society. The untrammelled human mind was to be the arbiter of truth, including the doctrines of religion, and a scientific, objective approach was called for in the study of music as of other matters. Johann Adolf Scheibe, whose name is chiefly remembered as the author of an attack on Bach, the last great master of abstract polyphony, defined the appropriate attitude of a mid-century composer thus: 'Musicians must think naturally and possess enlightened reason ... reasonable thinking and knowledge of the science of beauty create good taste in music.'

There was another force acting upon the Mozarts, father and son, which encouraged a rational, egalitarian approach to life and art. Freemasonry was established in Germany in the 1720s and spread rapidly among the bourgeoisie, though its influence was widespread too in aristocratic circles and even among the clergy, in spite of Pope Clement XII's edict of 1738 forbidding Catholics to join. Particularly strong in South Germany and Austria were the Masonic adherents known as 'Illuminati', whose aims were strongly ethical in character. Adam Weishaupt, their founder, went so far as to declare that 'Accumulated property is an insurmountable obstacle to the happiness of any nation', while a general Masonic aim was to 'combat superstition and fanaticism in the persons of the monkish orders, the main supporters of both these evils', possessed of 'a superfluity of goods'. Freemasonry was naturally regarded with a suspicion which often amounted to outright hostility by many church and state authorities, among them the ecclesiastical principality of Salzburg. There the Illuminati met by night in a lonely grotto at nearby Aigen, now known as the 'Illuminaten-Höhle'. Mozart attended some of these meetings, giving rise to the supposition that he may have been an Illuminatus. Certainly he followed his father by becoming a Freemason, a move which bore fruit in a number of works, above all *The Magic Flute*, whose story reflects Masonic rituals. In the later years of the eighteenth century, when democratic ideas exploded in the violence of the French

Revolution, Freemasonry, together with other 'enlightened' notions sharply lost favour in Austrian ruling circles, but at the time when Leopold Mozart entered court service at Salzburg, even the Prince himself, Baron Leopold Firmian, was suspected of Freemasonry (though it is difficult to see how this could be reconciled with his expulsion of 20,000 Protestants).

Firmian's successor, Count Jakob Ernst, was much given to entertainment, as was the man who followed him as Prince-Archbishop, Count Andreas Dietrichstein. Count Sigismund Schrattenbach, who took office in 1753, was a reformer who set about raising the moral tone in Salzburg, but fortunately for the Mozarts he was fond of music and treated them with easy-going indulgence.

Mozart's sister Maria Anna ('Nannerl'), who was born in July 1751 and outlived her brother by nearly forty years, listed in her memoirs the number of musicians in the employment of the Salzburg court. Apart from the Kapellmeister and his deputy there were 5 violinists, 2 cellists, 1 viola player, 2 bassoonists, 3 horns, 3 oboists, 3 flautists, 1 trumpeter and 2 organists – a chamber orchestra of moderate size. Music for the Cathedral was always in demand, so was background music for the dinner table, as well as music for more formal concerts and theatrical performances. Leopold Mozart, apart from his skill as a violinist, was adept, we are told, at composing works in every genre. Since music was at that time one of the chief means of entertaining and impressing state visitors, and since Leopold was allowed to write and perform for households other than the Archbishop's, he was a successful and very busy man when, on 27 January 1756, his wife Anna Maria gave birth to the second of their seven children to survive. He was christened Joannes Chrysostomus Wolfgangus Theophilus: Theophilus in its Latin form is Amadeus.

Chapter Two

A Prodigy of Nature
1756–1771

❋❋❋

The tourists who inspect Mozart's birthplace, No. 9 Getreide-gasse, walk in droves through a solidly built town house in a narrow, traffic-free street of prosperous shops. The house, formerly No. 225 and part of an elegant square which no longer exists, was the property of Johann Lorenz Hagenauer, a wholesale grocer, who leased his third floor to the Mozarts. Their quarters were modest but comfortable, and it was there, in a low-ceilinged room with a small window giving onto an inner courtyard, that the new baby was born.

Leopold lost no time in teaching his children music and in 1760 he made a note alongside the first eight pieces in Nannerl's music book that 'the preceding 8 minuets were learnt by Wolfgangerl in his 4th year'. The young boy's musical talent was not surprising, for his maternal grandfather, like his father, showed much aptitude for the art. From his grandfather, too, Wolfgang inherited a love of merriment which was not conspicuously present in Leopold, and all who knew the great composer as a young boy remembered his sense of fun.

'Before he began music', recalled Johann Andreas Schacht-ner, the court trumpeter, shortly after Mozart's death, 'he was so ready for any prank spiced with a little humour that he could quite forget food, drink and all things else.'

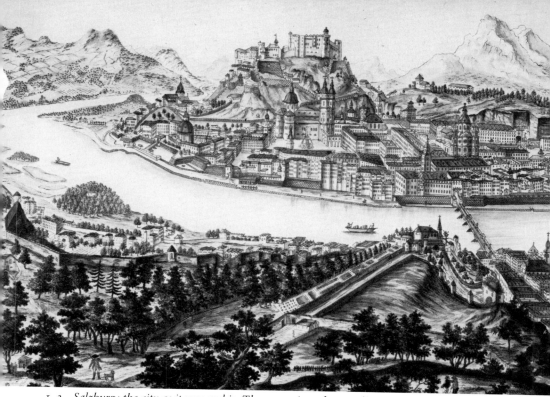

1, 2   Salzburg: the city as it was and is. The engraving of 1795 after a painting by Franz von Naumann and the twentieth-century photograph alike show the medieval castle dominating a concentrated array of imposing buildings.

3–6 A Mozart family group. Anna Maria Mozart (1720–1778) and her husband Johann Georg Leopold (1719–1787), 'the handsomest couple in Salzburg', with seven-year-old Wolfgang and his sister Nannerl wearing the gala costumes presented to them by the Empress Maria Theresa. The children's portraits were painted in 1763, probably by Pietro Antonio Lorenzoni.

7, 8 The Mozart family homes in Salzburg. Wolfgang was born on the third floor of what is now no. 9 Getreidegasse (right); in 1773 the family moved to much more spacious apartments (below) in the Hannibal-platz (now Makart-platz). Lithograph of Mozart's dwelling-house c. 1830, after Georg Pezolt

9 The elegant grandeur of Schönbrunn, the Imperial summer palace near Vienna, where Wolfgang, aged six, greatly impressed the Imperial family in October 1762. Helped up, after slipping on the polished floor, by Marie Antoinette, future Queen of France, Wolfgang is said to have asked her to marry him

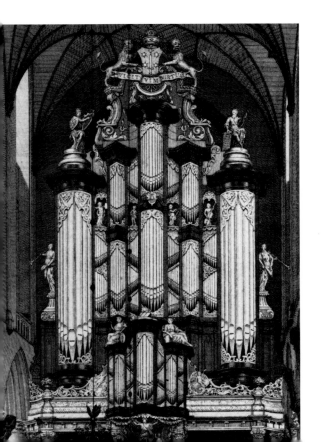

10, 11 Left: the Baroque splendour of the organ at St. Bavo, Haarlem, where the ten-year-old Mozart played in 1766. Organ by Christian Müller; engraving by Jan Caspar Philips, 1762. Above: Count Sigismund Schrattenbach (1698–1771), Prince-Archbishop of Salzburg from 1753. A moral reformer and, fortunately for the Mozarts, musical too.

12　*After their reception at Versailles on New Year's Day, 1764, the Mozarts were welcome in the grandest Parisian houses. Here Wolfgang plays the harpsichord during 'thé à l'anglaise' in the salon of the Prince de Conti; the Prince has his back to us. Painting by Michel-Barthélemy Ollivier, Paris 1766*

13　*The first violin part of a newly discovered childhood symphony of Mozart's, K.ANH.223 in F. In 1981 a full set of parts of this three-movement work, composed and probably performed during the Mozarts' visit to London in 1764–5, was found in Germany. Formerly it had been known only through fifteen bars jotted down and crossed out by Leopold, who saved money by acting as family copyist.*

14–16 *London as the Mozarts knew it.*
Above: *contemporary print of a royal
parade through from St James's Park.
Leopold was delighted when, on such an
occasion, King George III leaned out of his
carriage to wave to little Wolfgang.* Right:
*the house, now 180 Ebury St, where the
Mozarts lodged in August and September
1764.* Far right: *the Rotunda, Canal and
Chinese House at Ranelagh Gardens,
Chelsea, by C. Grignion after Canaletto.
Here, promised the* Public Advertiser, '*the
astonishing Master MOZART, lately arrived,
a Child of 7 Years of Age, will perform
several fine select Pieces of his own
composition on the Harpsichord and on the
Organ*'.

17, 18   Mozart's genius was widely recognized when he visited Italy in 1770 at the age of fourteen. Pope Clement XIV made him Knight of the Golden Spur (left: anonymous painting of 1777) and the influential Bologna musician Padre Martini (above) briefly gave him lessons.

19   In the Sistine Chapel (engraving by Francesco Barbazza after Francesco Pannini) Mozart heard Allegri's Miserere and subsequently wrote it out from memory.

The liveliness of his mind greatly impressed his sister Nannerl. 'He was desirous of learning everything he set eyes on', she wrote in later years: 'In drawing and adding he showed much skill, but, as he was too busy with music, he could not show his talents in any other direction.' Soon, it seems, music invaded his whole life: even children's games, according to Schachtner, 'had to have a musical accompaniment if they were to interest him; if we, he and I, were carrying his play-things from one room to another, the one of us who was empty-handed always had to sing or fiddle a march the while.' Wolfgang even invented a musical bedtime ritual which, according to Nannerl, he kept up until he was ten years old: 'he composed a melody which he would sing out loud each day before going to sleep, to which end his father had to set him on a chair. Father always had to sing the second part and when this ceremony, which might on no occasion be omitted, was over, he would kiss his father most tenderly and go to bed very peacefully and contentedly.'

It is clear that Mozart loved his parents, and particularly his father, very dearly. Affectionate as he was, he required constant assurances of love from others and if anyone teased him on the subject 'bright tears welled up in his eyes, so tender and kind was his heart'. Schachtner perceived that there were dangers in a temperament so mercurial: 'He was of a fiery disposition; no object held his attention by more than a thread. I think that if he had not had the advantageously good education which he enjoyed he might have become the most wicked villain, so susceptible was he to every attraction, the goodness or badness of which he was not yet able to examine.' The eagerness with which the eight-year-old Mozart left the harpsichord when a favourite cat came into the room, and the facility he showed for picking up card tricks and fencing tips from visitors when recovering from illness, though scarcely justifying the epithet 'wicked', bear witness to a nature wide open to distraction.

An understanding of Mozart in childhood is very relevant to his later development, for in the view of his sister 'he was, apart from his music, almost always a child, and thus he remained. This is a main feature of his character on the dark side. He always needed a father's, a mother's, or some other guardian's care: he could not manage his financial affairs.' Nannerl went on to say in her memoirs, perhaps unfairly, that he married a girl quite unsuited to him, and this led to the great domestic chaos at and after his death.

It is difficult to see how any wife could have matched the protective pride of the young Mozart's parents, from whom he inherited high intelligence but, it seems, little in the way of good looks. Leopold and Anna Maria had been known as the handsomest couple in Salzburg and Nannerl was considered a beauty. Wolfgang, however, was described by his elder sister, for all her devotion, as 'small, thin, pale in colour and entirely lacking in any pretentions as to physiognomy and bodily appearance'.

However, there is nothing to suggest that he was unfit for the rigours of Leopold's educational regime, which embraced many subjects apart from music, and the available evidence suggests that he enjoyed his early childhood. Though severe and demanding, Leopold greeted the growing evidence of Wolfgang's altogether exceptional talent with deep emotion, as the following incident shows.

Leopold was rehearsing some trios with two favoured colleagues from the court orchestra, Wentzel and Schachtner, when Wolfgang asked to be allowed to play second violin. Leopold refused, saying that he had not yet had the least instruction in the instrument. (Though Wolfgang must have been very young at the time, this statement may not have

*Autograph of the motet 'God is our Refuge', which Leopold presented to
the British Museum in 1765*

been absolutely true because we are told the boy was holding
'a little violin' at the time of the incident and went off with it
in a sulk.) Schachtner thereupon suggested he should be
allowed to play second violin along with him. 'Very well,' said
Leopold, 'but play so softly that we can't hear you or you will
have to go.' 'And so it was', Schachtner recalled to Nannerl,
'that Wolfgang played with me. I soon noticed with astonishment that I was quite superfluous. I quietly put down my
violin and looked at your papa; tears of wonder and comfort
ran down his cheeks.'

In 1761, Leopold was able to write alongside an Andante
and Allegro composed between February and April of that
year: 'Compositions by Wolfgangerl in the first three months
after his fifth birthday'. More wonder and comfort for the

proud father, who was already planning to make the great world aware of his clever offspring.

It would not have occurred to Leopold that there was anything wrong about exploiting the talents of Nannerl and Wolfgang. As Henry Raynor says in his book on Mozart:* 'Childhood as something different in nature from adulthood was the discovery of the early romantic movement. Leopold never realised, any more than did anyone in the eighteenth century, that children are not simply small adults.' Accordingly he planned a series of tours which would capitalize on the fashionable interest in prodigies of nature, convincing himself that, quite apart from any economic benefit which might accrue, it was his duty to 'prove the miracle' of his son's genius to the world in an age 'when everything called a miracle is ridiculed'.

To travel at all in those days required courage and endurance almost beyond our imagination, and it seems that conditions in Germany and Austria were the worst in Europe. Both the singer Michael Kelly and the musical scholar Charles Burney complained bitterly of the extortionate levies to which they were subjected – for the hire of vehicles and horses, tolls, turnpikes and the greasing of wheels, not to mention greasing the palms of ostlers 'who will steal any part of the luggage they can lay hold of'. Burney, like the Mozarts on their first journey, travelled by public conveyance and 'did not meet with a chaise or carriage that had a top or covering to protect passengers from heat, cold wind or rain; and so violent are the jolts and so hard are the seats of German post-wagons, that a man is kicked rather than carried from one place to another'. Michael Kelly, too, recalled a horrific journey by post-wagon: 'a complete bone-setter it was! While undergoing its operations, nothing could have so ably aided its torments as the unconquerable phlegm of the postillion.

* Macmillan, 1978

Legend:
- ·········· Grand Tour (1763–1766)
- ·–·–·– First Italian Tour (1769–1771)
- ++++ Tour to Potsdam and Berlin (1789)

ENGLAND
London
Amsterdam
The Hague
NETHERLANDS
Ghent
Brussels
BELGIUM
Lille
Aachen
Bonn
Cologne
GERMANY
POLAND
Berlin
Potsdam
Leipzig
Dresden
Prague
CZECHOSLOVAKIA
Paris
Frankfurt
Mainz
Mannheim
Schwetzingen
Stuttgart
Danube
Augsburg
Munich
Linz
Salzburg
Vienna
Bratislava
Dijon
Zürich
Berne
SWITZERLAND
Innsbruck
AUSTRIA
Danube
Geneva
Lyons
Milan
Verona
Venice
FRANCE
Parma
Bologna
Florence
ITALY
Rome
Naples

Mozart's Tours

Map showing the chief towns and cities visited by Mozart. The routes of
three important tours are indicated. The Grand Tour and first Italian tour
began from Salzburg, the German one from Vienna

Whatever one suffers, whatever one says, there he sits, lord
of your time.'

Germany and Austria at that time consisted of a large
number of small quasi-independent states like Salzburg, so
the Mozarts had a wide choice of potential markets. Leopold
chose Munich, in Bavaria, as his first objective, partly because
the Elector Maximilian Joseph III, who lived there, was a
musician himself, and partly because the distance was not too
great for what amounted to a trial run. Soon after Wolfgang's
sixth birthday, the whole family set out for the Munich
carnival season of 1762; few details of the visit have come
down to us, but we know the Mozarts were well received and
that Leopold made money.

He was sufficiently encouraged to plan a much more
ambitious journey in the autumn to Vienna, then of great
importance as the seat of the Imperial court and the capital
of the Holy Roman Empire. There the powerful Empress
Maria Theresa ruled with her consort, the Emperor Francis I;
the Seven Years War which was to establish Frederick the
Great's Prussia as a strong north German counterpoise to
Austria was nearing its end, so the court was no doubt glad of
entertainment and distraction – not that war in those days
seems to have seriously interfered with the social round
among the upper classes.

The family went first to Passau, where the important Count
Thun-Hohenstein was impressed but ungenerous, and from
there to Linz. Here Wolfgang gave his first public concert, in
October 1762. Fortunately, as Leopold wrote to his landlord
Lorenz Hagenauer, 'young Count Pálffy [nephew of the
Hungarian Chancellor] happened to be passing through
Linz as our concert was about to begin ... he listened with
astonishment and spoke later with great excitement of the
performance to the Archduke Joseph who passed it on to the

WASSER-ORDINAIRE

River travel in the eighteenth century

Empress.' So the ground was prepared for the Mozart's reception at court.

From Linz they continued their journey by mail boat down the Danube, experiencing violent storms. Let us hope they were better protected than Charles Burney who, in the course of his European journey a few years later, travelled down the Elbe in a boat which was 'long, narrow and quite open at the top. There was straw to lie on, but nothing to cover me or my baggage . . . about midnight it began to rain, after which the wind got up and became quite furious; in this kind of hurricane the boat could make no way. I was now wet, cold, hungry and totally helpless, for the boatman himself was in despair.'

The Mozarts arrived in Vienna safely on 6 October and were very soon engaged in an exhausting round of exhibition appearances at the houses of the nobility. This rose to fever pitch after their reception at the Imperial summer residence, Schönbrunn Palace, on 13 October: 'The nobles', Leopold told Hagenauer, 'send us their invitations four, five, six, to eight days in advance in order not to miss us.'

Though the Emperor was pleased with the young boy's performance on the harpsichord, he was not satisfied until he had produced such party tricks as playing with the keyboard covered over, and with one finger of each hand. Then followed a famous episode related thus by Arthur Hutchings:*

'The imperial family were evidently charmed by the children, for the empress Maria Theresa is said to have gone with some of her own children to show the little visitors the adjoining apartments. Wolfgang slipped on a polished floor, and the Archduchess Marie Antoinette, later queen of France, helped him up and received an immediate offer of marriage in return for her kindness. She was two months older than Wolfgang. Then, according to Leopold, "Wolferl jumped on the empress's lap, threw his arms round her neck and kissed her heartily".'

The visit to Schönbrunn lasted from 3 to 6 pm and one would have thought it enough for that day, especially for young children. However the prospect of six ducats from the Prince von Hildburghausen overruled fatigue and they drove straight to his house for the evening.

Handsome court dresses (which they subsequently wore for a portrait) soon arrived for Wolfgang and Nannerl from the Empress together with a hundred ducats and a pressing invitation to stay longer. Leopold was only too happy to comply with the Imperial suggestion, for it made his children the fashionable rage of Vienna.

At a concert in November, Leopold was handed the first poetic tribute to his son: 'On the little six-year-old clavier player from Salzburg'. With a reference to another child prodigy who had died young, it reads:

Child, worthy of our regard, whose ready skill we praise,
Who, small in stature, like the greatest plays;
For thee the art of sound will hold no pain,
Full soon wilt thou to mastery attain.
But may thy frame the soul's exactions bear,
And not, like Lübeck's child, too soon outwear.

* *Mozart: The Man, The Musician* (Thames and Hudson, 1976)

Such fears were well justified, for Wolfgang had already gone down, after his second visit to the Empress on 21 October, with a feverish illness which kept him in bed for some time. Leopold's sympathy was tempered with concern for his pocket: 'In Vienna', Hagenauer was informed, 'the nobility are afraid of pockmarks and all kinds of rash. So my boy's illness has meant a setback of about four weeks. Although since his recovery we have taken in twenty-four ducats, this is a mere trifle.'

A consoling profit resulted from a visit to Pressburg (now Bratislava) in December and Leopold was able to buy his own carriage, though this did little to soften the bumpy, frozen road 'full of deep ruts and ridges'. When they got back to Salzburg on 5 January 1763 after a brief return to Vienna, Wolfgang was again in bed for a week with rheumatism. However, he used his convalescence to perfect his violin playing, and his father – in spite of several months' absence – was gratified by promotion in February to the rank of vice-Kapellmeister.

We get an impression of Wolfgang's performances at this early age from a newspaper correspondent in Vienna. 'We fall into utter amazement', he wrote, 'on seeing a boy aged six at the clavier and hear him not by any means toy with sonatas, trios and concertos, but play in a manly way and improvise moreover for hours on end. . . . I saw them cover the keyboard with a handkerchief and he plays just as well. . . . Furthermore, . . . when he was made to listen in another room, they would give him notes . . . and he came out with the letter or the name of the note in an instant.'

Such was the degree of public interest that Leopold was very soon planning further travels – this time a Grand Tour which was to take the family away from Salzburg for almost three and a half years. They left on 9 June 1763 in their own carriage, which lost a wheel only two days later. The replacement did not fit properly and Leopold and the Mozarts' newly-acquired servant, Sebastian Winter, had to walk at times to ease the weight.

To list their innumerable stopping-places and all the tributes they received is beyond the scope of this book. The family travelled via Munich to Augsburg, where they 'stayed a long time and gained little or nothing': the children performed at the palace of Schwetzingen, country seat of Karl Theodor, the Elector Palatine and founder of the Mannheim orchestra, then considered the best in Germany. The teenage Goethe heard Wolfgang at one of the Mozarts' four or five concerts in Frankfurt: 'I saw him', he later recalled, 'when he was a seven-year-old boy. I myself was about fourteen years old and I can still quite clearly remember the little fellow with his wig and his sword.'

There were great hopes of Brussels, where the children did eventually appear before Prince Charles of Lorraine, brother of Emperor Francis I and governor of the Austrian Netherlands, but only after a wait of five weeks while the Prince pursued his customary diversions of hunting, eating and drinking; and the handsome presents bestowed on the family were no substitute for cash in hand.

In mid-November the family arrived in Paris, where they stayed with the Bavarian ambassador. Here again, everything depended on a successful royal reception. Owing to a period of court mourning, they did not go to Versailles until 24 December, where Madame de Pompadour impressed Leopold as 'an extremely haughty woman who still ruled over everything'. The children triumphed. Indeed, as Leopold put it, 'they took almost everyone by storm'.

There was an enforced pause, much regretted by his father, when Wolfgang developed a high fever in February 1764, but

Leopold felt he could look forward to 'a good harvest' after 'tilling the soil well'. In March the eight-year-old published his Opus 1 – two sonatas for the harpsichord (K6 and 7),* 'which can be played with violin accompaniment'. These were written no doubt with assistance from his father. Two more sonatas quickly followed and there were two profitable public concerts before the family left Paris in mid-April en route for England. 'I saw how the sea runs away and comes back again', observed Nannerl in her diary as they waited at Calais for the cross-channel packet.

The Mozarts were in London for fifteen months, from 23 April 1764 to 24 July 1765, lodging with a hairdresser off St Martin's Lane, and subsequently in Chelsea and Thrift (now Frith) Street, Soho. The first of three court appearances took place only five days after their arrival in the English capital and although 'the present was only twenty-four guineas', King George III and Queen Charlotte impressed Leopold by their 'easy manner and friendly ways' and the visit to Buckingham House had the desired effect of making the children fashionable everywhere. 'I have had the shock of taking one hundred guineas in three hours', Leopold exuberantly informed Hagenauer, his Salzburg landlord, after a benefit concert in June; but he also astutely realized that 'nothing wins the affection of this quite exceptional nation' more surely than charity work, so he let Wolfgang play the organ at a concert in aid of the newly-founded Lying-In Hospital 'in order to perform thereby the act of an English Patriot'.

Mozart dedicated his Opus 3 (K10–15) – a set of six sonatas 'for the harpsichord which can be played with the accompaniment of violin or transverse flute' – to the Queen and

---

* The K numbers in this book refer to the original edition of Köchel's index, rather than to the less familiar 6th edition published in 1964.

received a present of fifty guineas in reply. Further income was derived from putting Wolfgang on show at the family's Soho lodgings, where, as Leopold said in his advertisement, 'those ladies and gentlemen who will honour him with their company from twelve to three in the afternoon any day of the week except Tuesday and Friday may, by each taking a ticket, gratify their curiosity, and not only hear this young Music Master and his sister perform in private: but likewise try his surprising musical capacity'.

Among their visitors in June 1765 was a Fellow of the Royal Society, Daines Barrington, who, in a subsequent report, admitted being sceptical at first about the child's extreme youth. Although he had seen Wolfgang run about the room 'with a stick between his legs by way of a horse' and leave the harpsichord to play with his cat, Barrington carefully verified his age before expressing amazement at 'this prodigy of nature'. He submitted the boy to many searching tests, among them the instant composition of operatic arias to express Love and Anger. Mozart responded without difficulty, demonstrating 'a thorough knowledge of the fundamental principles of composition' and great facility in modulation: 'his transitions from one key to another were excessively natural and judicious'. As for Wolfgang's ability as a performer, Barrington declared that 'his execution was amazing, considering that his little fingers could scarcely reach a fifth on the harpsichord'.

Perhaps the most important musical encounter of the London visit was the young Mozart's meeting with Johann Christian Bach, the 'English Bach', son of the great Johann Sebastian and himself a fine composer in the urbane 'galant' style of the day. In her reminiscences, Nannerl describes how this important man shared a keyboard with Wolfgang one day: 'Herr Johann Christian Bach, the Queen's teacher, took

Wolfgang between his legs. The former played a few bars, and then the other continued, and in this way they played a whole sonata and someone not seeing it would have thought that only one man was playing.' J. C. Bach was a leading exponent of the newly-introduced fortepiano and may perhaps have sowed a seed which was later to grow into Mozart's great series of piano concertos. Certainly he was a strong influence on the boy's childhood compositions, which are sometimes indistinguishable from those of J. C. Bach.

Before the family left London, Leopold took care to present copies of his son's early works to the British Museum, in order to ensure that posterity would not forget the wonder he had produced.

Most of the remaining months of 1765 and the early part of 1766 were spent in the Netherlands, where the family travelled extensively and responded to an invitation to visit Princess Caroline of Nassau-Weilburg at The Hague. The Princess asked Mozart to write a set of sonatas to mark the coming of age and installation as Stadtholder of her brother, William V of Orange. There were also successful concerts in Amsterdam and many other places. But once again, towards the end of 1765, Leopold's plans had to be shelved because the children were ill, this time with intestinal typhoid. Nannerl at one point was given extreme unction and Wolfgang's life was in danger for some weeks.

In June 1766, the Mozarts were back in Paris, where they stayed for three days at Versailles. From there a slow homeward journey punctuated by frequent concerts and exhibition appearances took them back to Salzburg. Leopold and his family reached home on 29 November 1766.

The long and ambitious venture had been a financial success. The librarian of St Peter's Abbey in Salzburg expressed the belief 'that Herr Mozart's gewgaws, brought home by him,

The Prince-Archbishop, whose brother had provided inter-ludes of consoling hospitality during the Viennese sojourn, made up for the apparent indifference of the Imperial capital by ordering that *La finta semplice* should be performed on his name day. The Salzburg ruler had earlier put Wolfgang's powers as a composer to the test by shutting him up alone and making him set part of a church service, and towards the end of 1769 Wolfgang was given the title of third Konzertmeister of the Court Chapel. This would have involved composing as well as leading the court orchestra and was no doubt bestowed on the young musician to commit him firmly to Salzburg amid the temptations of the Italian journey his father was now planning. Italian credentials were highly desirable for an eighteenth-century musician, and for a budding opera composer it was necessary above all to succeed in Milan, as J. C. Bach had told Leopold in London.

Once again obtaining leave of absence from the Archbishop who must have been convinced that the Mozarts' successes abroad reflected credit on him, Leopold and Wolfgang set off accompanied by a servant on 13 December. Though he was now fourteen years of age, Wolfgang's slight build made him look younger – an impression fully exploited by Leopold – and his concerts in northern Italy in early January created immense interest. On the 23rd they arrived in Milan, where they were guests of Count Karl Joseph Firmian, nephew of the former Archbishop of Salzburg who first employed Leopold. Firmian was Governor-General of Lombardy, then under Austrian rule, and it was mainly through his powerful influence that all the right doors opened for the Mozarts, father and son, wherever they travelled on this Italian tour.

Letters home to Wolfgang's mother and sister tell us how things went. Many public and private concerts were arranged in Milan in the first three months of 1770, and for such grand

A decorative letter written from Milan by Leopold to his wife. Wolfgang often added obscene footnotes to Leopold's letters home. On this occasion he confined himself to the drawing (which includes an erotic message) and a chatty postscript (not reproduced here) to his sister

occasions, special clothes were required. 'The tailor has just called with cloaks and cowls which we have had to order', Leopold informed his wife in February; 'I looked at myself in the mirror as we were trying them on and thought of how, in my old age, I too have to take part in this tomfoolery.' If Leopold showed little respect in private for the grand people who patronized him, Wolfgang found relief from social solemnities by writing to his sister in a vein of lavatorial humour which continued to amuse him in later life. He told Nannerl of a dwarf he had seen in an opera at Mantua 'who jumps well but cannot write as I do, I mean as sows piddle'; and there was another in Cremona 'who, whenever he jumped, let off a fart'.

Apart from making Wolfgang's performing talent known to everyone who was anyone in Milan, Firmian made sure the boy was commissioned to write an opera for the next Christmas season. Thus it was with high hopes for the future as well as numerous letters of introduction that Leopold and Wolfgang set off for the south in March.

In Bologna, Wolfgang's abilities were tested by the influential musical scholar Padre Martini, whose expressions of admiration greatly enhanced the boy's reputation among Italians. In Florence there was a brief encounter with another prodigy, the English violinist Thomas Linley, who was Wolfgang's own age. The pair of them played duets and Wolfgang received a sonnet addressed to him on Linley's behalf. The boys clearly got on well, for Wolfgang later wrote to Linley in affectionate terms.

Soon after arriving in Rome, Leopold began to deliver 'twenty letters of introduction' which produced invitations to numerous palaces. Father and son went to hear the famous choir of the Sistine Chapel perform Allegri's *Miserere*, which was supposed to be their own closely guarded exclusive possession; and we are told that Wolfgang, deeply impressed, went home and wrote the whole piece out from memory – though it is just possible he had some prior knowledge of it. In other matters he was less well organized. 'Please try to find the arithmetical tables', he asked his sister in a letter; 'I have lost my copy and so have quite forgotten them.'

The road to Naples was at that time liable to attacks from brigands, and the city itself was far from salubrious: 'the lazzaroni have their own general', Nannerl was told, 'who receives 25 ducats from the King every month solely for keeping them in order'. Nevertheless the Mozarts were not deterred from visiting the southern capital where once again they enjoyed a huge success and found time for some sight-seeing. Leopold was impressed with the daily 'passeggio' of nobles taking their afternoon carriage drive; Wolfgang enjoyed watching Vesuvius 'smoking furiously' with 'thunder and lightning and all the rest'.

They were back in Rome at the end of June. Wolfgang had an audience of Pope Clement XIV, after having conferred on him a Knighthood of the Golden Spur, an exceptionally high honour for a musician. 'You can imagine how I laugh when I hear people calling him "Signor Cavaliere" ', wrote Leopold to his wife; but for all his amusement he can hardly have been less than gratified.

During a stay of three months in Bologna in the autumn, Wolfgang received the libretto and the list of singers for his Christmas opera *Mitridate, Rè di Ponto* (Mithridates, King of Pontus). In those days to please the 'prima donna' and 'primo uomo' was of the utmost importance and the young Mozart was brilliantly successful in this. By November he was hard at work in Milan and Leopold was able to report that 'the prima donna is infinitely pleased with her arias'. As for the primo uomo (a male soprano in the fashion of the time), he too was delighted and declared that if a certain duet did not succeed 'he would let himself be castrated again'.

The first performance of *Mitridate*, with Mozart directing a large orchestra from the keyboard, took place on 26 December 1770 to 'extraordinary applause and cries of "Evviva il Maestro! Evviva il Maestrino!"' After this triumph there was a highly successful visit to Venice for the Carnival of 1771 – Wolfgang was asked to write an opera for a future season and was received everywhere. Indeed, they did so much travelling by gondola that, said Leopold, 'during the first days the whole bed rocked in our sleep'. Then it was back via Innsbruck to Salzburg in March.

It was not long before Leopold and Wolfgang again set off for Milan, for the express purpose of carrying out a commission from the Empress Maria Theresa. Archbishop Schrattenbach once again gave permission but withheld Leopold's salary (it was ultimately paid to him, after Leopold petitioned the Cathedral Chapter 'but without precedent for the future, nor for other court musicians absenting themselves').

After a relatively rapid journey, father and son reached Milan in mid-August and soon Mozart was at work setting the libretto he had been given. *Ascanio in Alba* was completed in a month and given with the utmost success in October during the celebrations for the wedding of the Empress' son, the Archduke Ferdinand, to Princess Maria Ricciarda Beatrice of Modena.

The Mozarts were back in Salzburg again on 15 December 1771. The day after their return, the Prince-Archbishop, Sigismund Schrattenbach, died. Though latterly he had grown impatient with the prolonged absences of Leopold and his brilliant son, he had behaved towards them both with remarkable tolerance; over a period of nine years they had, after all, been away from Salzburg for almost seven. With the accession of Schrattenbach's successor there came a change of attitude which made life more awkward for the adolescent genius.

Chapter Three

Servitude and a
Bid for Freedom
1772–1778

❋❋❋

Mozart was now sixteen, well past the infant prodigy stage and already an accomplished composer with a large number of works of many different kinds to his credit. Leopold had taken care to give his son a thorough grounding in the theory and practice of composition and no opportunity had been missed during the family's extensive travels to meet and learn from the leading creative musicians of the day. Among them were Fux, Martini, Sammartini, Michael Haydn and, most important of all, Joseph Haydn, whose works were admired and most likely studied by Mozart before they met in 1781.

Wolfgang produced his first symphonies at the age of eight or nine under the influence of established composers in Paris and London in the course of the Grand Tour. Shortly after, he produced his first church music, a motet 'God is our Refuge' and a Kyrie (K33) for four voices and strings, continuing to compose a great deal of instrumental and vocal music apart from the stage works and other entertainments in operatic style which were his most spectacular successes to date.

Archbishop Hieronymus Colloredo, though he has come to be thought of as the villain of the piece in the Mozart story, was, by his own somewhat outdated standards, a fair-minded man. Rather stiff and formal, lacking in personal charm and very careful to preserve the hierarchical structure of a society in which musicians were merely servants, he nevertheless recognized Wolfgang's talent. Shortly after his appointment he commissioned the young man to write a dramatic serenata *Il sogno di Scipione* (Scipio's Dream) for his ceremonial installation in the Spring of 1772.

Charles Burney visited Salzburg that summer in the course of his 'Tour undertaken to collect Materials for a General History of Music' and reported that 'the archbishop and sovereign is very magnificent in his support of music, having usually near a hundred performers, vocal and instrumental, in his service. The prince is himself a dilettante and good performer on the violin; he has lately been at great pains to reform his band which has been accused of being more remarkable for coarseness and noise than delicacy and high-finishing.' Perhaps it was as part of the reforming process that Wolfgang was granted a yearly income of 150 florins in August as Konzertmeister or leader of the court orchestra. This was neither very generous nor unduly mean by the standards of the time and many musicians would have been content with such an appointment, carrying as it did the right to make extra money through teaching and other engagements, provided the Archbishop's requirements were met.

Wolfgang, however, had seen too much of the outside world to want to settle down indefinitely in Salzburg, and his father was eager for him to secure a more spectacular appointment than Colloredo could offer. Italy was particularly attractive, for there the young 'Cavaliere' was treated with respect, instead of having to defer obsequiously to others. Fortunately Wolfgang had been commissioned to write the first opera for the 1772–3 Carnival in Milan and in October Leopold and he set off southwards once again.

Lucio Silla was performed for the first time at the Teatro Regio Ducal on 26 December after the Archduke Ferdinand, delayed by official business, had kept everyone waiting for two or three hours. Such was the success of the opera that it was given no less than twenty-six times during the carnival season. Meanwhile Leopold persuaded Count Firmian to back an application to Archduke Leopold of Tuscany for a court appointment there for Wolfgang, and the two Mozarts lingered in Milan hoping for a favourable reply.

Wolfgang's mother and sister received reports of their doings in frequent letters which were partly written in cypher. Since the accession of Colloredo, the Mozarts had reason to suspect that letters might be intercepted and they naturally wished to keep discussion of possible new appointments from the Archbishop. Thus, to cover their delay in returning after the production of *Lucio Silla*, Leopold wrote in plain language to his wife in mid-January complaining that acute rheumatism had forced him to take to his bed. A week later followed another letter with a postscript in cypher which Anna Maria was instructed to cut off from the main text, saying that the story of his illness was a fabrication to put the Salzburg authorities off the scent; in fact they were still awaiting news from Florence. All Leopold's scheming was in vain, however, for no appointment was forthcoming and in March 1773 the travellers were back home in Salzburg. Shortly after their return they moved from the Getreidegasse to more spacious lodgings in the Hannibal-platz, now the Makart-platz, on the north side of the River Salzach.

Leopold and Wolfgang had little difficulty in obtaining further leave of absence from Colloredo in July since he himself was planning to be away. This time, in the secret hope of an appointment at the Imperial court, they returned to Vienna, but although they were received by the Empress, there

was no vacancy. Wolfgang occupied himself with the composition of a serenade (K185) and a set of six quartets (K168–
173), and the Mozarts renewed their friendship with Dr
Mesmer. Passing through Vienna on his way back to Salzburg,
the Archbishop extended their leave of absence, but he was
nonetheless lampooned in Wolfgang's letters to his sister 'from
our Residence, Vienna'. Reluctantly he and his father arrived
back in Salzburg on 26 September.

Whatever underlying hopes the young Mozart had of employment elsewhere, he now settled down to a period of over
a year in Salzburg in the course of which he produced many
beautiful works including a string quintet (K174 in B flat), his
first truly original piano concerto (K175 in D) and the Symphony in G minor K183, which resembles the great Symphony
no. 40 in little more than its key signature but all the same may
have surprised Salzburg by its intensity. In those days symphonies were often composed originally as extended opera
overtures and subsequently transferred from the theatre to
the salon. In that setting they were, like other 'chamber music',
thought of as charming entertainment, not to be taken too
seriously. Other fine symphonies of this period were the ones
in C major K200 and A major K201 – a particularly happy work
which has remained popular.

In 1774 the Elector of Bavaria commissioned Mozart to
write an opera for the forthcoming carnival season and early
in December Wolfgang arrived in Munich with his father to
supervise rehearsals. Colloredo was himself going to Munich
and so could hardly refuse permission; in the event *La finta
giardiniera*, which tells a romantic story about a young
countess disguised as a garden-girl, was a huge success which
can only have reflected credit on the Prince-Archbishop. There
were numerous encores on the first night, 13 January 1775,
and the opera was repeated several times in the course of the

season. Some of the concerted numbers in particular fore-shadow the incomparable operas Mozart was to create in the future.

Wolfgang reported his success in letters to his mother, adding: 'we cannot return to Salzburg very soon and Mama must not wish it, for she knows how much good it is doing me to be able to breathe freely'. Colloredo was once again the butt of uncharitable comments from Leopold, who asked Anna Maria to imagine 'the embarrassment of his Grace the Arch-bishop at hearing the opera praised by the whole family of the Elector and by all the nobles'; he also requested details of any Salzburg gossip about an appointment for Wolfgang in Munich: 'then we shall have something to laugh about, for we know these fools'.

Such rumours proved ill-founded, but, in the course of this Munich season, contemporary observers began to do justice to Mozart's rapidly growing stature as a composer. Of *La finta giardiniera*, the correspondent of an Augsburg journal wrote: 'flashes of genius appear here and there . . . if Mozart is not a plant forced in the hot-house, he is bound to grow into one of the greatest composers who ever lived'.

Whether Colloredo was quite so far-sighted in assessing his young employee's abilities is doubtful, but he very soon ordered Wolfgang to produce an operatic entertainment for the visit to Salzburg in April 1775 of the Archduke Maximilian. This was a setting of Metastasio's *Il rè pastore*, a story from classical antiquity about a defeated king who lives the life of a shepherd; it contains Mozart's first one-movement overture (in place of the three-movement 'sinfonia' which usually preceded operas in those days) and several beautiful arias and duets.

In the course of Maximilian's visit, Mozart was also called upon as a solo performer in his own instrumental compositions, and there is no evidence to suggest that during the two years he now spent at Salzburg he was not well appreciated. Among the many works he produced at this time were the *Serenata notturna* (K239), five violin concertos of which the last three are well-loved masterpieces, a triple piano concerto (K242) and the first great solo piano concerto, K271 in E flat. And for the wedding in 1776 of Elisabeth Haffner, daughter of the burgomaster of Salzburg, Mozart produced the nine-movement Haffner Serenade.

Wolfgang was still only twenty years of age and relished any opportunity for enjoyment which came his way. We get one glimpse of him relaxing in a description of a carnival party in February 1776 taken from the diary of Mozart's friend Joachim Ferdinand von Schiedenhofen, who became Court Councillor in Salzburg. 'At seven in the evening to the Master of the Household for supper', he wrote. 'Then in company to the rout, driving there with the Chief Equerry as a lady, the Marshal as a cavalier, Baron Lilien as a gallant, Count Micha as a courier, Herr Schmid as a hairdresser, the elder Mozart as a porter and the younger as a hairdresser's boy, Count Überacker as a moor and myself as a lackey. . . .'

The first sign of serious discontent with Salzburg which has come down to us is a letter Mozart wrote in September 1776 to Padre Martini, enclosing some church compositions for his perusal. Mozart complained of the restrictions of duration and personnel placed on his religious works, of the lack of good opera singers, of general parsimony; and he enlisted Martini's sympathy for his father who 'has already served this court for thirty-six years and, as he knows that the present archbishop cannot and will not have anything to do with people who are getting on in years, he no longer puts his whole heart into his work, but has taken up literature which was always a favourite study of his'. It seems that the Mozarts, in common with other resident Salzburg musicians, felt snubbed when the ruler closed his old theatre and ordered the construction of a new one – just opposite the Mozarts' new home as it happened – which would accommodate touring companies to the exclusion of the city's own performers.

In March 1777, the Archbishop rejected a request from Leopold and Wolfgang to go on a concert tour because the Emperor Joseph II was to visit Salzburg in July. On 1 August, the day after the Emperor departed, Wolfgang petitioned Colloredo for release from service on the grounds that 'The more of talent that children have received from God, the greater is the obligation to make use thereof, in order to ameliorate their own and their parents' circumstances, to assist their parents, and to take care of their own advancement and future.' 'To profit from our talents is taught us by the Gospel', the petitioner continued: an invocation of Divine approval echoed by the Archbishop, perhaps sarcastically, in a pencilled footnote to the Council decree agreeing to Mozart's request: 'Father and son herewith granted permission to seek their fortune according to the Gospel'.

Leopold, who had decided to remain behind, was allowed to continue in the Archbishop's service. But on 23 September Wolfgang set off with his mother in search of commissions and with the hope of a more substantial permanent appointment. From the family correspondence we get a vivid picture of what the journey meant both to the travellers and those they left behind at home.

Leopold found it hard to endure the day after the departure of his loved ones – 'that sad day which I never thought we should have to face'. Nannerl 'wept bitterly, complained of a headache and a sick stomach and went off to bed and had the shutters closed. Poor Bimbes [the dog] lay down beside her.' Eventually they found some distraction in the favourite family pastime of 'Bölzelschiessen' [shooting at a pictorial target with an airgun] but the absentees were by no means forgotten. The competitors shot on their behalf, with the result that 'Mama has won eleven kreuzer but Wolfgang has lost four'. Leopold was full of careful advice about good economical lodgings in his native city of Augsburg, but on the way there mother and son paused for three weeks in Munich. Here the Elector did not refuse Wolfgang an appointment outright, saying only that it was too early, that he ought to make more of a name for himself. Wolfgang toyed with the idea of getting ten friends to club together to maintain him for a while on a tight budget in Munich, but Leopold would have none of it: 'you must not make yourself so cheap and throw yourself away in this manner, for we have not come to that yet.'

On 11 October mother and son arrived in Augsburg, where the twenty-two-year-old composer was distracted from the serious business of making money (constantly urged on him in letters from home) by a lively cousin, Maria Anna Thekla, nicknamed 'the Bäsle' (little cousin). In an exuberant letter, Wolfgang described her to Leopold as 'beautiful, intelligent, charming, clever and gay. Indeed, we two get on extremely well for she, like myself, is a bit of a scamp. We both laugh at everyone and have great fun.' The letter goes on to describe a concert where many of the nobility were present: 'the Duchess Smackbottom, the Countess Makewater, to say nothing of Princess Dunghill with her two daughters who, however, are already married to the two Princes Potbelly von Pigtail. I kiss Papa's hand 100,000 times and embrace my brute of a sister with bearish tenderness.'

Leopold's letters betray an increasing irritation with his son's tendency to be distracted from the matter in hand; exasperation at the younger Mozart's lack of practical sense and his careless approach to correspondence is almost always

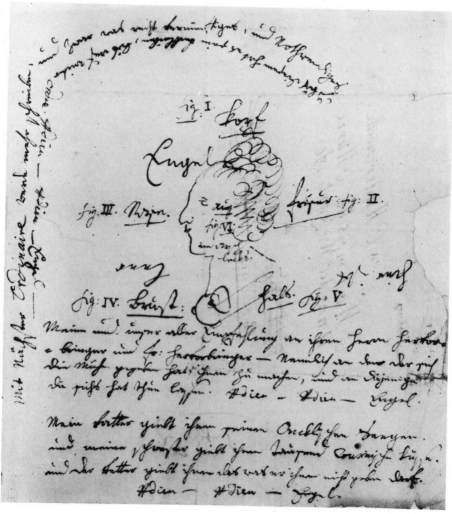

Letter to his cousin, 'the Bäsle', dated 10 May 1779. The writing up the side and round the top reads: 'I shall write more by the next "Ordinaire" post – and I promise that it shall be something very sensible and important, and we must just be content with that until further notice.' On the drawing itself, Mozart has written 'fig. I: head, fig. II: hair, fig. III: nose, fig. IV: breast, fig. V: neck'. By the forehead is written 'angel'

evident: 'many of my questions receive no answer; on the other hand you will notice that I reply to all yours'.

Apart from 'the Bäsle', Wolfgang's main source of interest in Augsburg was the piano maker Andreas Stein, whose instruments he greatly admired. He played them in public too. As one Augsburg newspaper put it: 'The evening of Wednesday last was one of the most agreeable for the local music lover. Herr Chevalier Mozart, son of the famous Salzburg musician who is a native of Augsburg, gave a concert on the fortepiano in the hall of Count Fugger. As Herr Stein happened to have three instruments of the kind ready, there was an opportunity to include a fine concerto for three claviers.' The programme also included a number of other works by Mozart. 'One thing gave relief to another, so that the numerous assembly was displeased with nothing but the fact that the pleasure was not prolonged still further.' Although his reputation was enhanced, Wolfgang was dissatisfied with the cash profit of his stay in Augsburg, and by the end of October he and his mother were in Mannheim, seat of the Elector Palatine, Karl Theodor, whose large orchestra had an expressive range unrivalled in Europe.

Soon Mozart was attending rehearsals with the orchestra's leader, Christian Cannabich, who – Wolfgang informed his father – 'has taken a great fancy to me. He has a daughter who plays the clavier quite nicely and in order to make a real friend of him, I am now working at a sonata for her.' By no means forgetful of his own abilities and earlier triumphs, Wolfgang was amused by the way the Mannheim musicians reacted to him. 'I thought I should not be able to keep myself from laughing when I was introduced to the people there. Some who knew me by repute were very polite and fearfully respectful; others, however, who had never heard of me, stared at me wide-eyed, and in a rather sneering manner. They probably think because I am little and young, nothing great or mature can come out of me; but they will soon see . . .'

Early in November, Mozart made a great impression at a concert in the presence of the Elector and Electress, but the only tangible reward was 'a fine gold watch. At the moment', he told his father, 'ten carolins would have suited me better than the watch which, including the chains and the mottoes, had been valued at twenty. What one needs on a journey is *money*; and let me tell you, I now have *five* watches! I am therefore seriously thinking of having an additional watch pocket on each leg of my trousers, so that when I visit some great lord I shall wear watches on both sides, which moreover is now the "mode", so that it will not occur to him to present me with another one.'

Leopold, now aged fifty-eight, and, by his own account, in debt despite rigorous domestic economies, categorically agreed. 'It would have been very much better', he commented, 'if you had received fifteen louis d'or instead of a watch. . . . For the love of God, you really must try to get some money . . . you must see to it that the Elector of *Mainz* hears you play and that you receive a present of money.'

But Wolfgang had decided to remain in Mannheim for the winter. His vague hopes of a court appointment were backed by Leopold in a letter to Padre Martini requesting a testimonial; but nothing happened. It is, after all, possible that the Elector Karl Theodor – who early in January 1778 also became Elector of Bavaria – was reluctant to employ one whose behaviour towards a fellow ruler could be interpreted as desertion. Whatever the reason, Mozart found little response from the Mannheim court, though he and his mother were kindly treated by others.

A Privy Councillor eventually took them into his own home after Frau Mozart had suffered much discomfort in dreary lodgings. There, she told her husband, she was often alone, and had to put up with 'the most horrible cold. For even if they light a small fire, they never put any more coal on it, so that when it burns out the room gets cold again. A little fire of this sort costs twelve kreuzer. So I make them light one in the morning when we get up and another in the evening . . . as I write I can hardly hold my pen, I am freezing so. . . .' Wolfgang was often out with friends, occasionally with practical results. 'He lunched today with a wealthy Dutchman', Anna Maria wrote, 'who is giving him two hundred gulden for some compositions.'

These were 'three short concertos and a couple of quartets for the flute' but to his father's unbridled fury Wolfgang only received 96 gulden, since he failed to complete the commission. He was never very interested in the flute; but there was another reason for his inattention to work.

In January 1778 he became acquainted with a small-part singer at the court theatre, Herr Fridolin Weber, and was soon in love with his seventeen-year-old daughter, Aloysia, who, Leopold learned, 'sings admirably and has a lovely pure voice. The only thing she lacks is dramatic action; were it not for that she could be a prima donna on any stage.' And Mozart promptly formulated plans to further her career by travelling with the family to Italy. They would go via Salzburg, an idea which probably raised Frau Mozart's hopes of an early return home. If so, she reckoned without the thunderous response of her husband: 'I am quite willing to believe', he wrote, 'that Mlle Weber sings like a Gabrielli; that she has a powerful voice for the Italian stage; that she has the build of a prima donna but . . . what impresario would not laugh were one to recommend to him a girl of sixteen or seventeen who has never appeared on a stage . . . as for your proposal (I can hardly write when I think of it) – your proposal to travel about

*Silhouette of Aloysia Weber,
Mozart's first love,
by Löschenkohl*

with Herr Weber *and*, be it noted, his *two daughters* – it has nearly made me lose my reason . . . could you *really* make up your mind to go trailing about the world with *strangers*? Quite apart from *your* reputation, what of your *old parents* and your *dear sister*?'

Such wild notions aside, Mozart had been seriously contemplating a visit to the French capital, where he had enjoyed such prodigious success as a child, so he was inclined to respond to his father's brisk injunction: 'Off with you to Paris! Find your place among great people. From Paris the name and fame of a man of great talent resounds throughout the whole world. There the nobility treat men of genius with the greatest deference, esteem and courtesy.' And Leopold was skilful enough to produce an argument which may have clinched the matter. 'Win fame and *make money* in Paris. Then, when you have money to spend, go off to Italy and get commissions for operas. This cannot be done by writing to impresarios. Then you could put forward Mlle Weber's name, which can more easily be done if you do so personally.'

In March, Mozart and his mother set off on the nine-day journey to Paris. They went in their own carriage but only because they had promised to sell it to their coachman on arrival. It was an inauspicious start to the saddest episode so far in Mozart's life.

Very soon Wolfgang began to look up the long list of contacts his father had given him, but in a city the size of Paris it was not that easy, now that they had no private means of transport. 'You say that I ought to pay a good many calls in order to make new acquaintances and revive the old ones. That, however, is out of the question. The distances are too great for walking – or the roads too muddy, for really the mud in Paris is beyond description. To take a carriage means that you have the honour of spending four to five livres a day, and all for nothing. People pay plenty of compliments it is true, but there it ends. Paris is greatly changed; the French are not nearly as polite as they were fifteen years ago.'

No doubt the Parisians had found a brilliant little boy of seven far more amusing than an ambitious young man of twenty-two. Fortunately Mozart had at least one influential supporter, Baron Melchior von Grimm, who had done a great deal to promote the interests of the family during their first visit to the French capital. He now sent Wolfgang on the rounds of his aristocratic friends. Let us hope he was sometimes received with more courtesy than the Duchesse de Chabot offered. In her house, Mozart wrote, 'I had to wait for half an hour in a large ice-cold unheated room that hadn't even a fireplace. At last the Duchess appeared. She asked me to make the best of the clavier in that room as none of her own were in good condition. I said that I should be delighted to try it, but that it was impossible at the moment as my fingers were numb with cold. "Oui, Oui, monsieur, you are quite right" was all the reply I got. She then sat down and commenced to draw, having as company some gentlemen who all sat in a circle round a big table while I had the honour to wait. There was total silence and I did not know what to do for cold, headache and boredom. At last I played on that miserable wretched pianoforte. But what vexed me most of all was that madame and her gentlemen never interrupted their drawing for a moment, so that I had to play to the chairs, tables and walls.'

Meanwhile Mozart's mother sat at home in the poor lodgings they had taken for the sake of economy. 'The room is dark', she told Leopold, 'and looks out on a small closed yard. I can neither see the sun nor tell what the weather is. And for this we have to pay thirty livres a month!' Anna Maria complained to her husband about the food and the high prices in Paris and he sympathized, suggesting she should try to find someone who cooked 'in our German way', but he was unable to help with money. If life was hard in Paris, it was chaotic in Austria, where 'there is no talk of anything but the delivery of horses and the transport of food. . . . people are being whipped off the streets and pulled out of their beds to be turned into soldiers. For heaven's sake use patience', Leopold once again implored his son, 'and exert yourself!'

Since his lodgings had no piano, Wolfgang was already spending his days at the house of Jean le Gros, director of the Concert Spirituel. He planned a sinfonia concertante for four Mannheim players who were in Paris (their instruments were flute, oboe, horn and bassoon) but if Mozart ever wrote it, Le Gros failed to have it copied and it was not included in the concert where it was supposed to be performed. 'Something is going on behind the scenes' was Mozart's suspicion: 'if this were a place where people had ears to hear, hearts to feel and some measure of taste for music, these things would only make me laugh heartily; but as it is, so far as music is concerned I am surrounded by brute beasts.' One of his trials was giving lessons in composition to the daughter of the Duc de Guines, 'a stupid and lazy girl' who 'had not an idea in her head'; what is more, he was kept waiting for his fees. Music lovers, however, gained from this unhappy experience since Mozart composed for father and daughter the Flute and Harp Concerto (K299), which is among his most beloved works.

In April 1778, things improved somewhat for the young composer and his mother. New lodgings were found for them which were altogether more congenial and contained a piano. Anna Maria was unwell for a time but her health improved. Wolfgang was offered the post of organist at Versailles, though Grimm advised against acceptance, realizing that composition was the young man's chief love.

On 18 June the Concert Spirituel opened with a magnificent symphony by Mozart known to us as the 'Paris', K297. He was bitterly disappointed with the playing at rehearsal and almost decided to stay away from the concert itself. However, at last he made up his mind to go, 'determined that if my symphony went as badly as at the rehearsal I would make my way into the orchestra, snatch the fiddle out of the hands of Lahoussaye and conduct myself.' In the event, all was well and the Parisians liked the piece . . . 'particularly the last Allegro, because having observed that all *last* as well as *first* Allegros begin here with all the instruments playing in unison, I began mine with two violins only, piano for the first eight bars followed instantly by a forte. The audience, as I had expected, said "hush" at the beginning and when they heard the forte at once began to clap their hands. I was so happy that as soon as the symphony was over I went off to the Palais Royal where I had a large ice and said the rosary as I had vowed to do.'

Opening of the 'Paris' Symphony, K297. *Mozart flattered Parisian taste with his opening unison tutti, the* coup d'archet

Mozart gave his father this cheering news in a letter written at a moment of tragedy. On the day after the success of his symphony, Anna Maria had taken to her bed with a chill. Poorly nourished on cheap food and short of proper medical attention she rapidly got worse and on 3 July she died. Sitting by her bedside, Wolfgang could not bring himself to tell Leopold the bitter truth, saying only that his mother was very ill and that he had resigned himself wholly to the will of God. By the same post he begged a Salzburg friend, the Abbé Bullinger, to break the news to his father 'very gently. May God give him strength and courage.'

Wolfgang soon learned that Leopold and Nannerl were heartbroken and was reminded by his father, as if his own awareness were not sufficient, of the sacrifices his mother had made for him. At home the court organist, Anton Adlgasser, had died and there was reason to think Wolfgang could have the post if he returned forthwith to Salzburg. There were grounds for hope that permission for worthwhile travel abroad would not be withheld.

Mozart resisted. 'If I were to undertake the work, I should have to have complete freedom of action. The Chief Steward should have nothing to say to me in musical matters, or on any point relating to music. For a courtier can't do the work of a Kapellmeister, but a Kapellmeister can well be a courtier.' To Bullinger he wrote of 'the injustices which my dear father and I have endured at Salzburg which in themselves would be enough to make me wish to forget the place and blot it out of our memory forever.'

So Wolfgang remained in Paris for three further months, staying with Baron Grimm and Madame d'Épinay. A hoped-for commission from the Opéra did not materialize. As 'an act of friendship' he composed some music (*Les Petits Riens*) for the ballet master Noverre, which was used in a totally forgotten piece by Gluck's rival Piccinni, and he waited with impatience for the proofs of six violin sonatas from a publisher.

Meanwhile Grimm, who had lent Mozart money, aroused the young man's resentment by reminding him of his obligations and wrote pessimistically to Leopold about prospects in France for one who was 'too generous, not pushful, too easily deceived' and altogether lacking in the 'craft, enterprise and boldness' required for wordly success. On 26 September he was packed off for home on a coach which 'crawled at a snail's place'.

Mozart himself was still in no hurry. After giving poorly attended concerts in Strasbourg, he returned to Mannheim, where he stayed for a month, in the hope of a theatre commission. Then he went to Munich where Karl Theodor had now transferred his court, his orchestra and his opera, which meant that the Weber family were installed in the Bavarian capital.

There, Aloysia was enjoying some success as a singer and spurned the renewed advances of Wolfgang, whose future at that stage seemed to hold little promise, though this blow was softened to some extent by the presence in Munich of the cheerful 'Bäsle', who eventually accompanied Mozart back home. After presenting Karl Theodor's wife, the Electress Maria Elisabeth, with the violin sonatas which had been engraved in Paris, Wolfgang and his cousin left Bavaria and reached Salzburg on 15 January 1779.

Chapter Four

The Final Break
1779–1781

❊❊❊

On his return to Salzburg, Mozart was appointed Court Organist and he remained at home for the best part of two years, carrying out the duties required of him by the Prince-Archbishop.

It was probably for a ceremony in the Spring of 1779, during which a crown was placed on a statue of the Virgin at the Church of Maria Plein on the outskirts of Salzburg, that Mozart wrote the Coronation Mass in C major, K317; for the Cathedral he composed two settings of the service of Vespers and added to an earlier series of 'epistle sonatas' for organ and strings: they were so named because they were performed between the readings of the epistle and Gospel. Three symphonies date from this period – K318 in G, a short but spirited work, K319 in B flat for small orchestra and K338 in C, which has an andante movement of exceptional beauty. Perhaps the most splendid of all the Salzburg works is the Sinfonia Concertante for violin, viola and orchestra, K364, which introduces a profundity new to the young composer, still only in his early twenties.

Apart from composing and performing, Mozart was required as Court Organist to give keyboard lessons, so he was very fully employed during these two years spent at home with his father and sister. Meanwhile his reputation in the world outside Salzburg continued to grow, if slowly. The *Mercure de France* praised Mozart's symphonic style for its richness in ideas, adding, however, that it appealed more · strongly to the mind than the heart. In the Spring of 1780, *La finta giardiniera* was given in German at Augsburg – probably the first time that an opera of Mozart's was given on a stage other than the one for which it was written. But in the same year any lingering hopes Mozart may have entertained about Aloysia Weber were finally extinguished when she married the court actor Josef Lange in Vienna, and the routine of life at Salzburg became increasingly irksome to him, as we learn from the letters he wrote after leaving the city in November 1780 to complete an opera commissioned by the Elector Karl Theodor for the forthcoming Carnival season in Munich.

Mozart had begun work on what was to be the first of his great operas well before he left Salzburg, for the Court Chaplain there, Gianbattista Varesco, had been commissioned to provide the libretto. Once established in Munich, Mozart found it necessary to make many alterations to suit the talents of his singers and he was also at pains to simplify the text and make it more dramatically effective. Leopold Mozart acted as intermediary in a lengthy and acrimonious correspondence with Varesco, who eventually became very angry and demanded a higher fee. Since he had been asked to produce no less than four versions of the text and a good many additional alterations, he perhaps deserved better than to be dismissed by Leopold as 'a greedy, money-grubbing fool'. However, while keeping Varesco up to the mark, Leopold also treated his son to a torrent of advice. 'You must note all the [textual alterations] in your copy immediately, so that when you are composing the music, none of them may be overlooked', Wolfgang was told; he was also warned, when composing, 'to consider not only the musical but the un-musical public. You must remember that to every ten real connoisseurs there are a hundred ignoramuses. So do not neglect the so-called popular style which tickles long ears.' There was also guidance about how to treat the orchestra in Munich: flattery was recommended as a specific for getting through long rehearsals, when the humblest viola player was as much in need of a pat on the back as anyone else.

It was left to Leopold to explain matters to the Archbishop when the six-week leave he had granted to Wolfgang ran out in mid-December, before rehearsals for the opera had even begun. There seems to have been no great pressure on him to return, but that did not prevent Wolfgang abusing his master in coded sentences, of which the following gives some idea: 'If only the Ass who smashes a *r*ing and by so doing *c*uts himself a *h*iatus in his *b*ehind so that *I* hear him *s*hit like a castrato with *h*orns and with his long ear *o*ffers to caress the fox's *p*osterior, were not so . . ., why, we could all live together.'

Mozart's sister Nannerl occupied part of her time sitting for a joint portrait with Wolfgang, who had himself been painted for the picture during the previous summer, and in mid-January she set out with their father for Munich, where they arrived in time for the dress rehearsal of *Idomeneo* on Mozart's birthday, 27 January. On the 29th, after two postponements, the first performance took place, to immense acclaim.

Idomeneo belongs to that well-defined genre of eighteenth-century theatrical entertainment, the *opera seria*. That is to say, it tells a story of classical antiquity in a manner akin to that of classical tragedy, which admits no light relief. Such pieces had often been loaded with irrelevant divertissements before the time of Gluck, who introduced a simpler, more dignified presentation in which every musical number was necessary to the unfolding story. Mozart, in his arguments with Varesco, was trying to achieve a similar effect.

The work which resulted is both powerful and passionate. It is the story of a King of Crete at the time of the Trojan wars. Praying to the sea-god for delivery from a storm at sea, he promises to sacrifice the first living thing he meets on shore. Unfortunately, he is greeted by his son Idamante. A monster which ravages the island when Idomeneo evades his vow is killed by Idamante, who, when he learns of his father's promise, offers himself as a sacrifice. At the last moment the voice of the sea-god is heard, sparing Idamante on condition that Idomeneo abdicates. Idamante becomes king, with Ilia, the woman he loves, as his consort. Among many splendid arias is Idomeneo's 'Fuor del mar', designed as a display piece of coloratura brilliance for Anton Raaff, the sixty-six-year-old tenor who created the part at Munich.

After he had seen his opera successfully staged, Mozart was still in no hurry at all to return to Salzburg. He stayed on to make the most of the Carnival season in Munich and paid a family visit to Augsburg with Nannerl and Leopold. Only after an absence of four months did Mozart pay heed, in mid-March, to the Archbishop's orders to join his household forthwith in Vienna. Colloredo had gone there to wait on Emperor Joseph II, who, following the death in November 1780 of Maria Theresa, now ruled alone, and to be near his ailing father, the Imperial Vice-Chancellor.

Required to perform on demand as a clavier player, Mozart was given 'a charming room' in Colloredo's house, but the domestic arrangements were not to his liking. 'The two valets sit at the top of the table', he wrote home, 'but at least I have the honour of being placed above the cooks. I almost believe myself back in Salzburg!' Clearly Mozart had learned something from his father's tactics with fellow servants, for he added 'A good deal of silly, coarse joking goes on at the table, but no one cracks jokes with me, for I never say a word, or, if I have to speak, I always do so with the utmost gravity and as soon as I have finished my lunch, I get up and go off.' After his big success in Munich, it is easy to understand how deeply Mozart must have resented his return to servitude, underlined by the fact that others, like the orchestra leader Brunetti and the singer Ceccarelli, were allowed the freedom of choosing their own lodgings.

When the Archbishop's musicians gave a concert at the house of Prince Galitzin in March 1781, Mozart snubbed his colleagues by going there alone, and when he arrived, he walked straight up to the Prince and engaged him in conversation, leaving Ceccarelli and Brunetti to hover uncertainly behind the orchestra, 'not daring to come forward a single step'. According to his own account, all the nobility of Vienna had taken Mozart's part against the Archbishop when permission was refused for Mozart to appear at a charity concert for the Wiener Tonkünstlersocietät; however, at Prince Galitzin's soirée, Colloredo changed his mind. The result was a big triumph for Mozart at the Kärntnertor Theatre in April. But causes of resentment continued to multiply. On the very night when he might have been playing before the Emperor for a big fee at Countess Thun's, Mozart was required for a concert at the house of Colloredo's father, and, worse still, the Archbishop refused permission for Mozart to give a public concert which he believed would be very profitable. He wrote to his father: 'When I think that I must leave Vienna without bringing home at least a thousand gulden, my heart is sore indeed. For the sake of a malevolent Prince who plagues me every day and only pays me a lousy salary of four hundred gulden, am I to kick away a thousand? For I should certainly make that sum if I were to give a concert.'

At this stage, although toying with the possibility of an independent career, Mozart still intended to return to Salzburg when the Archbishop's visit to Vienna was over and improvised variations on a theme proposed by Colloredo at a farewell concert in Vienna at the end of April. However, when the Archbishop tried yet again to put Mozart down by ordering him to take back a parcel to Salzburg forthwith, the patience he was endeavouring to show for the sake of his father finally cracked. Wolfgang refused the commission, saying he needed to remain in Vienna for a few days to collect money owing to him. Bidden to leave Colloredo's house at once, he took refuge with the Webers. On 9 May, he had an open row with the Archbishop. 'Well, young fellow,' Colloredo began, 'when are you going off?' Mozart said he could not go that day, making the transparent excuse that the coach was full. The Archbishop told him he had better go that day or he would have his salary stopped; Mozart was 'the most dissolute fellow he knew, no one served him so badly'; he was 'a scoundrel, a rascal, a vagabond'. Pleading for his father's understanding, Mozart's letter home continued: 'Then my blood began to boil, I could no longer contain myself and I said "So your Grace is not satisfied with me?" "What, you dare to threaten me? . . . There is the door! Look out, for I will have nothing more to do with such a miserable wretch." At last I said "Nor I with you!" "Well, be off!" When leaving the room I said "This is final. You shall have it tomorrow in writing!"'

The following day Wolfgang tried to return to Count Arco the money he had been given for the journey and to hand in a petition for dismissal, but the diplomatic Arco told Mozart he should not take such a step without consulting his father. A week later another similar interview followed. Sensibly, Arco told Mozart that if he remained alone in Vienna he could not expect the fickle Viennese to support him for long, that he should stop giving the Archbishop the impression that he was 'insufferably insolent' and swallow his pride. But that was not Mozart's way. 'I treat people as they treat me' was his reply. 'When I see that someone despises me and treats me with contempt, I can be as proud as a peacock.'

The final break came early in June. Once again Arco refused to accept Mozart's petition, and no doubt exasperated by the pressure put on him by the Archbishop, by Leopold and by the young man himself, shoved him out of the door with a kick. 'So that's the way to win people over, to soften them up!' wrote Mozart. 'Throwing them out of doors with a kick on the behind. That's the style!'

Now aged sixty-one, Leopold feared not only for his son's future but his own, since Wolfgang was threatening revenge on Arco, summing up his courageous if foolhardy attitude with the words: 'Although I am not a count, I have more honour in my heart than has many a count. Lackey or count, whoever insults me is treated by me as a rascal.' Feeling that he had finally thrown off his fetters, Mozart now abandoned the use of cypher in letters home, though there is evidence that from time to time they were still read by Colloredo. To such a man, Mozart must have seemed intolerably arrogant: 'I am more respected in Vienna than the Archbishop', claimed Wolfgang. 'He is only known as a presumptuous, conceited ecclesiastic who despises everyone here, whereas I am considered a very amiable person.'

As Mozart set out to make a life for himself in Vienna, he begged his father not to worry about his prospects. 'I have here', he wrote, 'the finest and most useful acquaintances in the world. I am liked and respected by the greatest families.' Then, as now, good contacts were vital to the success of a free-lance musician, and the more aristocratic they were in

Imperial Vienna the better. The Emperor Joseph II has been described as the most thorough of the enlightened despots of the eighteenth century. A declared enemy of superstition and outmoded tradition, he sought to create a strong centralized state out of the disparate territories and nationalities over which he ruled. He promoted religious toleration, relaxed censorship and encouraged education, and although the total effect of his reign was to leave the Hapsburg Empire in greater turmoil than before, Vienna in the early 1780s was a stimulating place for a rising young artist.

Believing in the stage as an instrument of propaganda, Joseph decreed that the Burgtheater should become a national theatre with the object of bringing unity through culture to his diverse subjects. Though now banished to the suburbs, the popular theatre, stimulated by the spirit of rivalry, flourished as never before under the leadership of such men as Karl Marinelli, who built a new theatre at Leopoldstadt, and Emanuel Schikaneder, the future librettist of Mozart's *The Magic Flute*, and already the most popular and accomplished theatrical figure of his time in Austria.

In 1780 Vienna was a city of 175,000 people which had doubled its population in forty years, a prosperous and cosmopolitan centre which flourished despite a series of wars in which Austria was often defeated. Though the majority of people were fervent Catholics, freemasonry was spreading rapidly and the absence of censorship allowed a stream of outspoken pamphlets to appear with such titles as *Is the Emperor Right?* and *The Degradation of the Lay Clergy*. On a more popular level there was the anti-clerical *Mamma wants to send me to a convent*!

Self-denial was out of fashion in a city denounced by some visitors for its excessive love of pleasure, a taste which matched in extravagance the decorative exuberance of

Viennese Baroque architecture. Approaching Vienna from the river in the course of his Musical Tours, Dr Charles Burney was impressed by the 'forty or fifty towers and spires' which rose above the city, and although he found that the streets were 'rendered doubly dark and dirty by their narrowness and by the extreme height of the houses', he thought the houses themselves were 'grand and magnificent in appearance' thanks to their 'elegant style of architecture in which the Italian taste prevails, as in music'.

It was a city where music abounded at all hours of the day and night. A band of 'French horns, clarinets, hautboys and bassoons', though 'miserably out of tune', serenaded Burney during meals and in the evening at his inn, *The Golden Ox*; one Sunday morning he was stopped in the street by a procession 'three miles long, singing a hymn to the Virgin in three parts', and he was surprised to hear even the soldiers on guard singing together in harmony. Innumerable festivals gave rise to dancing in the public pleasure gardens which, in any case, according to a visitor from Berlin in 1781, were always full of working-class people after five in the afternoon. As for their 'betters', they were not slow to subscribe to a forthcoming series of concerts provided the musician concerned was able to catch the popular fancy.

Mozart was right in thinking that if any city in the Europe of his time could give him a living, it was Vienna.

20   *Munich, where Mozart appeared before the Bavarian Elector in 1762, and later scored successes with* La Finta Giardiniera *(1775) and* Idomeneo *(1780). Engraving of 1761 after Bernardo Bellotto.*

21   *Above: Hieronymus Colloredo, successor to Schrattenbach as Prince-Archbishop of Salzburg. Authoritarian perhaps, but not quite the intolerant tyrant of Mozart's letters.*

22   *Right: Mozart's first love, the singer Aloysia Weber, whose sister, Constanze, he eventually married. The 1784 engraving by Johannes Esaias Nilson shows Aloysia as Zémire in Grétry's* Zémire et Azor.

23 Above: Paris, a view
towards the Notre Dame
bridge, 1782. Tramping
through the mud of the busy
streets in 1778, Mozart
found little to remind him of
his childhood triumph in the
French capital.

24 Left: The Redoutensaal
in Vienna's Hofburg,
engraving by M. Weinmann,
1748. Scene of happier
moments for Mozart: he
attended a masked ball here
in 1786 dressed as an Indian
guru, and as Court
composer often wrote dance
music for Redoutensaal
festivities.

25 Right: Baron Melchior
von Grimm (wash drawing
by Louis Carrogis de
Carmontelle, 1758). Grimm
tried to help in Paris but
found Mozart obstinate and
naive.

26–28 Mozart's marriage took place on
4 August 1782 at Vienna's St Stephen's
Cathedral. The posthumous oil portrait by
Barbara Krafft (left) dates from 1819 but
was painted under Nannerl's supervision
and is thought to be one of the best
likenesses of the composer as a young man.
He was twenty-six when he married

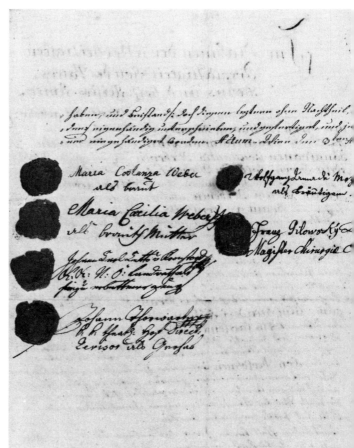

Constanze Weber (right: oil painting by Joseph Lange, who married Aloysia Weber). Mozart had convinced himself that Constanze was 'the gentlest, cleverest and best' of the Weber girls. Below: the marriage contract, ultimately signed on 3 August 1782, after a certain amount of Weber family pressure.

In Nahmen der allerheiligsten Dreyfaltigkeit, Gott des Vaters, Sohns, und heil: Geistes Amen.

29–33 *Mozart's Vienna and some notable contemporaries.* Top: *Vienna as seen by Bellotto, 1759–60. Left foreground, Schwarzenberg Gardens; to the right, gardens of the Belvedere Palace; St Stephen's Cathedral is in the middle distance. Portraits (from left to right): 30 Antonio Salieri (1750–1825), lithograph of 1815. Italian composer and one of Mozart's more successful rivals, but hardly likely to have poisoned him, as rumour suggested. 31 Muzio Clementi (1752–1832). Italian composer and pianist, highly regarded*

by Beethoven but dismissed by Mozart as a mere mechanical wonder, after their performing contest in 1781. 32 Christoph Willibald Gluck (1714–1787). After operatic triumphs in Paris, Gluck became Court composer to the Austrian Emperor and lived opulently in Vienna. 33 Joseph Haydn (1732–1809) depicted at the age of sixty-seven in an oil portrait by J. C. Roesler (1799). The revered Haydn's example and encouragement were of great value to the much younger Mozart.

34, 35 *The egalitarian principles of Freemasonry strongly appealed to Mozart, who was elected apprentice at the Viennese lodge 'Beneficence' when he was twenty-nine. Above: anonymous painting of the 1780s, showing a meeting of a Masonic lodge in Vienna. The figure seated on the far right is believed by some authorities to be Mozart. Left: a fellow-Mason, Count Thun, surrounded by Masonic symbols. The rituals of Freemasonry strongly influenced the story of* The Magic Flute.

Chapter Five

Success in Vienna
1781–1786

❊❊❊

Mozart's life as a free-lance musician began modestly enough. In June 1781 he apologized to his father for sending him only 30 ducats because so far he had only one pupil and could 'only just make both ends meet'. But before the end of the month he was engaged to teach the daughter of an Economic Counsellor, Josepha von Auernhammer, a lady of influence as well as musical talent; the only difficulty here was that she was ugly ('as fat as a farm wench', said Mozart) and that she fell in love with her teacher.

The unattached Wolfgang attracted any number of rumours about his amorous activities, many of them circulated by dedicated enemies such as the Czech clavier player Leopold Kozeluch, who was no doubt jealous of Mozart's talent, and who preserved his own reputation by playing in public as little as possible. One Herr von Moll expressed the hope that Mozart would soon return to Salzburg as he was 'only in Vienna for the sake of the women', and further scandal was caused by his continued residence at the Weber's, where it was supposed he was too intimately involved with Aloysia's sister Constanze. Wolfgang felt it necessary to deny all these allegations firmly in letters home to his father, asserting in July 1781 that he was only just beginning to live and that God had not given him his talent 'that I might attach it to a wife and waste my youth in idleness'. Mozart left the Webers, lodging briefly with the Auernhammers – a move hardly likely to improve his reputation in view of Josepha's known feelings – before taking a room on his own in the inner city.

The year 1781 brought the publication of six sonatas for clavier and violin, and in July Mozart received the libretto for a play with music in the German tradition (Singspiel), from Gottlieb Stephanie, dramatist at the Burgtheater. This was *Die Entführung aus dem Serail* (The Abduction from the Seraglio), an entertainment strongly laced with the fashionable Turkish flavour, intended for a forthcoming state visit, though in the event, production was delayed until the following year. Meanwhile personal problems continued to worry the young musician.

In December, despite his former resistance to the notion of 'settling down', he broached to his father the idea of marriage. He had never been one, he said, to seduce innocent girls, but 'the voice of nature speaks as loud in me as in many a big lout of a fellow'; moreover, he had never been accustomed to look after his own belongings – 'linen, clothes and so forth' – and was convinced he could 'manage better with a wife' even on his existing income. Mozart was doing his best to rationalize a situation he could not avoid, for such was the gossip involving his name with that of Constanze Weber that the Weber's family guardian extracted a promise from him to marry Constanze within three years, in default of which he would have to make her a handsome annual allowance.

At the end of 1781, while these problems were still unresolved, Mozart took part in a keyboard competition before the Emperor at the Hofburg. His opponent, the acclaimed virtuoso and composer Muzio Clementi (1752–1832), spoke of Mozart, who was regarded as the winner, in generous terms, but Wolfgang was less charitable. He dismissed

The Burgtheater announces the first performance of The Seraglio *on 16 July 1782*

Clementi as 'a charlatan, like all Italians. . . . His greatest strength lies in his passages in thirds. Apart from this he has not a kreuzer's worth of taste or feeling – in short he is simply a mechanicus'.

Mozart's constant hopes for an appointment at court were in no way advanced by the competition, though he was well paid for taking part in it. During the early part of 1782, however, he gave an important concert at the Burgtheater and helped to inaugurate a subscription series in the Augarten. July brought the first performance at the Burgtheater of *Die Entführung*. It is said that the Emperor, who was present, remarked that the opera had 'very many notes', to which Mozart replied 'exactly the right number, your Majesty'. Although both the first and second performances provoked a certain amount of hissing from cabals organized by Mozart's enemies, the work was a success from the start. Gluck, the most respected operatic composer in Vienna at the time, requested an extra performance, and in the world outside Vienna, *The Seraglio* was to become the most successful of all Mozart's stage works in his lifetime.

It tells the story of a lover, Belmonte, who rescues his loved one, Constanze, together with her English maid and Belmonte's servant from the harem of a Turkish Pasha. The Pasha, though in love with Constanze, magnanimously forgives them in the end. There is much superb music for the principal characters, including Constanze's great aria 'Martern aller Arten', and the piece owes a great measure of its popularity to the Pasha's comic servant Osmin, a character who obviously appealed to Mozart, for he requested his librettist to enlarge the part.

No sooner was *The Seraglio* launched than Mozart implored his father to give consent to his marriage with the real-life Constanze: 'my heart is restless and my head is confused; in such a condition how can one think and work to any good purpose?' On 3 August the marriage contract was signed, and the day after, the couple were married in St Stephen's Cathedral. The Baroness von Waldstädten gave a 'princely' supper for them, Gluck invited the young couple to dinner and Leopold's consent arrived, a little late but nonetheless received with great relief by Wolfgang: 'I kiss your hands and thank you with all the tenderness which a son has ever felt for a father, for your kind consent and fatherly blessing.'

That Leopold was still far from happy about his son's welfare is made clear in a letter to the Baroness, begging her to keep an eye on Wolfgang. 'Two opposing elements rule his nature', said Leopold. 'There is either too much or too little, never the golden mean. If he is not actually in want, then he becomes indolent and lazy. If he has to bestir himself, then he realizes his worth and *wants to make his fortune at once.* Nothing must stand in his way; yet it is unfortunately the most capable people and those who possess outstanding genius who have the greatest obstacles to face.' It also appears from this letter that the elder Mozart was being victimized in Salzburg for his son's behaviour towards the Archbishop, though Leopold did his best to come to terms with his situation: 'I live quietly with my daughter and have a few friends who come to see me. Reading, music and an occasional walk are our recreation and in bad weather a very humble game . . . of chess.'

The pressure surrounding his marriage in no way blinded Wolfgang to Constanze's good qualities – her common sense and kind heart outweighing an absence of wit and a tendency to extravagance – and he was eager to take his new wife to Salzburg to meet his father and sister. Mozart started work on the grandest of all his settings of the Mass – in C minor, K427 – with the intention of having it performed during this projected Salzburg visit. No one knows exactly why the work was never completed but perhaps it was because the start of a new season in Vienna held out the promise of more pupils and concert opportunities, and for the time being the visit was postponed. There was, besides, the possibility of a permanent appointment as music master to the Princess of Württemberg: Mozart had been recommended by the Archduke Maximilian and had to mask his disappointment when the post went to Georg Summer, clavier instructor to the Imperial Court. He was able to convince himself that his income from pupils already matched the salary he might have expected from the Princess.

However, the need to make money by teaching became increasingly irksome to Mozart, for it took time which might have been devoted to his 'beloved composition'. He had to complete three piano concertos, apart from writing a good deal of small-scale instrumental music and dance music, and these marked the beginning of one of his finest achievements as a composer: the series of great dialogues for piano and orchestra which virtually created the piano concerto as we know it. The concertos in F, A and C (K413, 414 and 415) were described by Mozart as 'a happy medium between what is too easy and too difficult; they are very brilliant, pleasing to the ear and natural, without being vapid. There are passages here and there from which connoisseurs alone can derive satisfaction; but these passages are written in such a way that the less learned cannot fail to be pleased, though without knowing why.' The three concertos were published in the winter of 1782, at a time when his reputation stood high as 'one of the greatest virtuosi in Europe'. 'At his incomparable pianoforte', wrote a member of the audience at an Augarten concert of this period, 'he several times caused us to feel sweet enchantment and the admiration due to him for his brilliant performance.' Nor was Wolfgang's fame confined to Vienna; in March 1783, a Hamburg music magazine indicated his standing when it predicted that the thirteen-year-old Beethoven was 'sure to become a second Wolfgang Amadeus Mozart if he progresses as he has already begun'.

The newly-married couple were able to move into progressively better lodgings, eventually attaining the coveted status of a first-floor apartment in April 1783. During the Carnival season that year, they had given an all-night ball in a house in the Wipplingerstrasse where they were staying at the time, though when writing to Leopold for the loan of his Harlequin costume, Wolfgang took care to inform his father that he had made the gallants pay for the privilege of attending his party. However, whether that was the case or not, it seems

A ticket for a concert given by Mozart c. 1784–5

the Mozarts were already living beyond their means, for in the Spring of 1783 Mozart asked the Baroness von Waldstädten for a loan to settle a debt.

To all appearances, Mozart was doing well. In March 1783 he took part in a concert arranged by his sister-in-law, Aloysia Lange, at the Burgtheater; it was attended by Gluck, who warmly praised Mozart's Symphony K297 (the one he had written in Paris) and invited the Mozarts and Langes to his home. A fortnight later Wolfgang was gratified by the presence of the Emperor at a concert of his own in the same theatre. It was a resounding success; the Emperor was delighted, and Mozart believed he might have been even more generously rewarded if the Imperial gift of money had been made after the concert, instead of being deposited at the box office beforehand, as the custom was.

In May, the question of a visit to Salzburg was again discussed, but as Mozart had never been officially dismissed by the Archbishop he thought he might be arrested when he got there. His situation in Vienna was altogether different; when the Mozart's first child was born in June, Baron Wetzlar offered to stand godfather, though this caused a passing difficulty with Mozart senior. Wolfgang had fully intended to name the boy Leopold, but just before the christening, Wetzlar kissed the child and said 'so now you have a little Raimund' (the name of the Baron's eldest son). Mozart felt he could not offend his patron, so Raimund Leopold it had to be.

Leopold had dismissed as 'mere humbug' Wolfgang's fears about returning to Salzburg, and the young couple had set off in July for their long-promised visit to Mozart's native city. Parts of the incomplete C minor Mass were performed during the visit at St Peter's Church, according to tradition with Constanze as soprano soloist, but the three-month family reunion was only a qualified success and on 27 October the young Mozarts left to return to Vienna via Linz, where they spent three weeks as guests of Count Thun. Mozart was asked to give a concert in the theatre, for which a major work was required, but this placed him in a difficulty. 'As I have not a single symphony with me', he told Leopold, 'I am writing a new one at breakneck speed.' This was the Symphony in C, K425, now known as the 'Linz'.

Back in Vienna, where baby Raimund had died in his absence (from intestinal cramp), Wolfgang entered on the most flourishing period of his life. In the year 1784 he was in constant demand for concerts, giving no fewer than nineteen in the month of March alone. He was also composing at a feverish rate, so the Mozarts' domestic regime was severe; they were never in bed before midnight, and up at five or half past five most mornings; no wonder the maid they had brought with them from Salzburg complained of lack of sleep. The first report of Mozart's poor health dates from this period of excessive activity: in the summer he suffered what was probably a kidney infection, with violent bouts of vomiting.

During that year Mozart produced six of his finest piano concertos, one of which, K449 in E flat, he sent to his father in February, asking him not to show it to a single soul. Wolfgang had composed it for the daughter of a court councillor and been well paid – a much better arrangement, in Mozart's view, than giving his work to an engraver who would then swindle him by 'printing off as many copies as he likes'. He formed the intention of publishing in the future only by collecting subscribers in advance; the large number of people who were willing to subscribe for his concerts seemed a promising augury.

Apart from concertos, Mozart was producing music of several other kinds at this time, including works for one and two pianos, three superb wind serenades and a number of other chamber works including the six string quartets he dedicated to Haydn, which were published in 1785. These works – dialogues between four instruments of equal importance – were written under the influence of Haydn's own quartets, particularly those of op. 33, which are notable for their contrapuntal integration of four independent parts.

Mozart probably met Haydn in 1781 and a friendship grew up between them which was furthered by the quartet parties in which they both participated. The singer Michael Kelly referred to one such party at the house of the English composer Stephen Storace in 1784 when 'the players were tolerable; not one of them excelled on the instrument he played, but there was a little science among them, which I daresay will be acknowledged when I name them:

The First Violin . . . . HAYDN.
  „ Second Violin . . . . DITTERSDORF.
  „ Violoncello . . . . VANHALL.
  „ Tenor [viola] . . . . MOZART.'

*Title-page of the six string quartets dedicated to Haydn
and published in Vienna in 1785*

The 'Haydn quartets' were the result of 'long and laborious endeavour' on the part of Mozart, eager as he was to please the dedicatee. As for Haydn, his admiration for Mozart was unbounded, and it is pleasant to record that Wolfgang's father was able to experience this outstanding testimony to his son's success at first hand.

In August 1784, Wolfgang's sister Nannerl married a government official at St Gilgen, Johann von Berchtold zu Sonnenburg. Just before the event Wolfgang wrote to her, expressing the brotherly hope that the letter would reach her while she was still a Vestal Virgin – 'another few days and . . . it is gone!' 'Our only regrets', he added in the same letter, 'are for our dear father who will now be left so utterly alone.' One palliative, Mozart knew, would be to invite his father to Vienna, where he would be in his element helping to organize the incessant round of concerts.

Leopold reached Vienna on 11 February 1785, and the day after his arrival he joined Wolfgang and two other players in performing three of the 'Haydn quartets' in the presence of Haydn himself. It must surely have been gratifying when he heard from Haydn's own lips on this occasion the famous declaration: 'Before God and as an honest man, I tell you that your son is the greatest composer known to me either in person or by name. He has taste, and what is more, the most profound knowledge of composition.'

So much for a great fellow-composer's seal of approval. As for the popular view of Mozart at this time, we can gain some idea from Schink's rather gushing *Literary Fragments* published in Graz: there Mozart is praised as 'great and original in his compositions, and a master when seated at the keyboard. His Concerto on the Piano-forte, how excellent that was! And his improvisations, what a wealth of ideas! What variety! What contrasts in passionate sounds! One swims away with him unresistingly on the stream of his emotions.'

Predictably, Leopold was delighted by the acclaim which greeted his son wherever he went and by the money which appeared to be flowing in. A month after he arrived he told Nannerl in a letter that 'since my arrival your brother's forte-piano has been taken at least a dozen times to the theatre or some other house'. He rubbed his hands over the takings at a major concert in the Burgtheater on top of the proceeds from six subscription concerts, and offered the opinion that 'if my son has no debts to pay, I think he can now lodge two thousand gulden in the bank. Certainly the money is there, and so far as eating and drinking are concerned, the housekeeping is extremely economical.'

Just before his father arrived in Vienna, Wolfgang was elected to the Masonic lodge 'Beneficence' as an apprentice, but very soon advanced beyond this lowest of grades. In March 1785, Leopold was admitted to the same lodge and made even more rapid progress, being promoted from apprentice to master in little more than two weeks. This unusual haste was caused by Leopold's imminent departure from Vienna. For once following his son's example, he had overstayed the six weeks leave of absence granted him by the Archbishop, and under the threat of having his salary stopped if he stayed away any longer, he left for home on 25 April.

There now followed a period when Mozart's letters to Salzburg were fewer and further between. In November, Leopold complained to Nannerl that he had not heard from his son for a month; shortly afterwards he received a few lines giving the reason, or at any rate one reason: he was 'up to the eyes in work on *Le nozze di Figaro*, and Leopold was understanding enough to realize that 'there will be a lot of running about and discussions before [Wolfgang] gets the libretto so adjusted as to suit his purpose exactly, and no doubt according to his charming habit, he has kept on postponing matters and has let the time slip by.'

Mozart could not really afford to concentrate on composition at the expense of performing. Though we have Leopold's word for it that Constanze's housekeeping was not lavish, the couple did consider it indispensable to keep up appearances, and the struggle to make ends meet became ever more difficult. In November 1785, Mozart implored the composer and publisher Franz Anton Hoffmeister to help out with some money 'which I need very badly at the moment'. At about this time he drove himself to prepare three new piano concertos for the Lent concert season of 1786, while devoting most of his energy to his latest operatic venture, *The Marriage of Figaro*.

Exactly how Mozart came to decide on this subject is not clear. He had read through a large number of plays and had even begun to set one by Lorenzo da Ponte, the poet to the Imperial Theatres in Vienna; this subject, *Lo sposo deluso* (The Deceived Husband), was soon abandoned, probably on account of the weakness of the libretto. In January 1785, the Emperor instructed the censor to ban from the Viennese stage Beaumarchais's wittily subversive play *Le mariage de Figaro* 'since this piece contains much that is objectionable'. But the play, though not performed in Vienna, was printed, and from this Mozart and da Ponte fashioned a piece from which the politically offensive material was removed without making the characters into spineless puppets. Endowed with a ceaseless flow of Mozart's finest music, *Figaro* is one of the greatest and most human of all operatic comedies.

It is a story of intrigue in an aristocratic household. The Count is attracted by his wife's maid Susanna, who is betrothed to the valet Figaro, though Figaro in turn has to get out of an obligation to marry someone else. The page Cherubino is banished to the army by the Count for excessive flirting; the Countess is distraught because she thinks she has lost her husband's love. After many ingenious twists and turns, everyone's problems are resolved, thanks to the ready wit of the plebeian Figaro rather than good sense on the part of his social superiors.

Silhouettes by Löschenkohl of the first performers of The Marriage of
Figaro. *From left to right: Nancy Storace (Susanna), Stefano Mandini
(Count Almaviva), Maria Mandini (Marcellina), Michael Kelly (Don
Basilio and Don Curzio), Francesco Benucci (Figaro), Francesco
Bussani (Antonio)*

Mozart needed all the persistence he could command to get
his new opera produced. The tenor Michael Kelly tells us that
works by Gluck and Righini were awaiting production at
much the same time and cabals were feverishly active in
support of Mozart's rivals. Finally a decree from the Emperor
himself settled the matter: *The Marriage of Figaro* was to be
put into rehearsal forthwith. Perhaps Mozart had won a good
measure of Imperial favour through the one-act opera *Der
Schauspieldirektor* (The Impresario) he had composed for a
private festivity at Schönbrunn in February 1786 – though he
received only half as much money as his rival Salieri did for
another piece given on the same occasion.

The first night of *The Marriage of Figaro* on 1 May 1786
at the Burgtheater must have been a real success, for practically
every number was encored and the opera lasted nearly twice
as long as intended. The effect of this was an Imperial ban on
encores for ensemble pieces 'to prevent the excessive duration
of operas', in its way a compliment to *Figaro*. There were

technical problems on the first night and perhaps it took a little time for Vienna fully to take the measure of the new opera, as a Viennese newspaper report of July 1786 suggests: 'Herr Mozart's music was generally admired by connoisseurs already at the first performance, if we except only those whose self-love and conceit will not allow them to find merit in anything not written by themselves. The public, however (and this often happens to the public), did not really know on the first day where it stood. But now after several performances, one would be subscribing either to the cabal or to tastelessness if one were to maintain that Herr Mozart's music is anything but a masterpiece of art.'

If Mozart had been living today, he would have been well rewarded for his masterpiece with royalty payments and all kinds of other spin-offs. In the Vienna of those days he received a single payment of 450 gulden which was no more than he might have got from a successful concert, and did very little to delay the onset of chronic insolvency.

95

Chapter Six

Public Acclaim, Private Misery 1786–1790

Although *Figaro* was given eight further performances in Vienna in 1786, none was for the composer's benefit, so Mozart began to think of further tours abroad as a source of income. Italy was considered, so was England – a project abandoned when Leopold flatly refused to look after his son's surviving children. For the rest of the year Mozart remained in Vienna, producing a series of fine chamber works, the great C major Piano Concerto K503 and the Symphony in D K504, which became known as the 'Prague'.

The music-loving public of the Bohemian capital had been strongly aware of Mozart's music since a production there of *The Seraglio*; soon after *Figaro* had been staged in Vienna, rehearsals began for a production of the opera in Prague, and by mid-December the city's newspapers were full of reports of its runaway success. 'No piece', wrote one observer, 'has ever caused such a sensation'; after several performances the theatre was still full and a 'positive rain' of complimentary German poems was thrown down from the gallery.

36 *Perhaps the most romantic of Mozart portraits, though unfinished. It was painted by Aloysia's husband Joseph Lange at about the time of Mozart's marriage to her sister Constanze, when Mozart was twenty-six. It is interesting to compare this with the posthumous portrait ill. 26.*

37, 38 *The Emperor Joseph II, who succeeded to the throne in November 1780. In many ways an enlightened ruler, he made the Vienna of his time a stimulating place for creative artists. Painting by Pompeo Batoni, 1769. Below: print by Johann Ziegler of the Lindenallee in the Augarten. Formerly belonging to the emperor's residence at Leopoldstadt, the garden was opened to the public by Joseph II, after which it became the Viennese counterpart of the famous Vauxhall pleasure gardens in London.*

39, 40　*Vienna, a rooftop view of the Inner City with the dome of St Peter's Church and the spire of St Stephen's Cathedral. Right: Peter Shaffer's highly acclaimed play* Amadeus *portrays Mozart as gauche and foul-mouthed. Salieri basks in public approval but bitterly realizes he cannot match Mozart's genius. Frank Finlay (left) and Richard O'Callaghan as Salieri and Mozart.*

41, 42 *Autograph manuscript of
Cherubino's aria 'Non so più' from* The
Marriage of Figaro. *The Beaumarchais
play on which the opera was based was
banned from the Viennese stage for all
the Emperor's enlightenment, but
Lorenzo da Ponte* (right: *engraving by
Michele Pekenino after a painting by
Nathaniel Rogers) contrived to fashion a
libretto which was witty without being
subversive.*

43, 44   *The interior and exterior of the original Burgtheater, Vienna, built between 1741 and 1756. The 1789 engraving of St Michael's Square by Carl Schütz shows the Burgtheater on the extreme right. Mozart gave numerous concerts in this theatre and three of his operas were first performed there.*

45, 46 Left: *watercolour by Karl Postl (1769–1818) of Prague, looking towards the castle, Cathedral and the Charles Bridge.* Mozart enjoyed two triumphant visits to Prague in 1787, the second for the première on 29 October of Don Giovanni. Opposite below: *a modern interpretation of Don Giovanni. The masked figures of Donna Anna, Donna Elvira and Don Ottavio in Joseph Losey's film of the opera which was set against the Palladian architecture of Vicenza.*

47 *Interior of the Villa Betramka, Prague.* Wolfgang and Constanze lived here for part of the time during Mozart's second visit to Prague in 1787.

48 In this house, standing in what was then the suburban Landstrasse, Mozart lived from April to December 1787, when working on Don Giovanni. The house no longer exists. On 4 June Mozart buried in the garden the starling he had bought for 34 kreuzer three years earlier.

49 Mozart's piano by Anton Walter, which now stands in the birthplace museum. Mozart bought the instrument in 1784 and fitted it with a special sustaining device.

When news of such a success was followed by an invitation to stay at Count Thun's palace in Prague, the Mozarts hesitated no longer. They set off soon after Christmas and arrived on 11 January 1787 to a gratifying reception. On the very evening of their arrival, Mozart went to a ball given by a wealthy member of the aristocracy, Baron Bretfeld, where the beauties of Prague, according to the composer, 'flew about in sheer delight to the music of my *Figaro* arranged for quadrilles and waltzes. . . . Nothing is played, blown, sung or whistled but *Figaro*.' On 17 January, Wolfgang's presence at a performance of the opera was greeted by ecstatic applause as soon as the overture was finished; he directed the next performance himself from the keyboard, after a concert in the theatre the previous day which included the 'Prague' symphony and a full half-hour of improvisation from the maestro, including, by insistent popular request, variations on the hit tune of the day, Figaro's aria 'Non più andrai'. Mozart's triumph was complete. In the words of one newspaper, the *Prager Oberpostamtszeitung*, 'everything that was expected of this greatest artist was fulfilled to perfection'.

Before returning to Vienna in February 1787, Mozart had been commissioned by Bondini, the manager of the Prague theatre, to write a new opera for the following season, and he at once requested Lorenzo da Ponte to provide another Italian libretto.

The Venetian-born poet, at this time in his late thirties and destined to survive till he was nearly ninety, was in great demand. At almost the same moment he was asked for libretti by Mozart, Salieri and Vicente Martín y Soler, whose opera *Una cosa rara* had enjoyed a success rivalling that of *Figaro* the previous year. Da Ponte claimed to have assured a sceptical Emperor that he could cope with all three at once: 'I shall write at night for Mozart', he said, 'and count that as reading

Dante's *Inferno*. I shall write in the morning for Martín, the equivalent of studying Petrarch. The evening will be for Salieri, and that will be my Tasso'. If we are to believe da Ponte's memoirs, he settled down to work with a bottle of Tokay and 'a pretty sixteen-year-old girl (whom I had wished to love only as a daughter, but . . .). She came into my room at the sound of a hand-bell, which, to be truthful, rang a great deal: she fetched me now a biscuit, now a cup of coffee, now nothing but her own pretty face, perfectly fashioned to arouse poetic inspiration and the witty idea.'

For personal or other reasons, da Ponte was drawn to the Don Juan story and created a version of it for Mozart based on Goldoni's *Don Giovanni Tenorio* of 1736 and a more recent libretto by a Venetian rival called *Il convitato di pietra* (The Stone Guest). From this treatment of the story, da Ponte borrowed the appearance of the avenging statue of the Commendatore which brings about the final destruction of the libidinous Don, and provided Mozart with a magnificent dramatic opportunity. But he also allowed the composer's genius ample scope in other ways, for example with the contrasting characters of three of the Don's victims, Donna Anna, Donna Elvira and the peasant girl Zerlina. There was light relief in the character of the servant Leporello, and material for the magnificent ensemble sequences which are among the glories of *Don Giovanni*.

The creation of the new opera was Mozart's chief pre-occupation during 1787, though he also found time for other works, among them the string quintets in C major and G minor (K515 and 516) and the A major Violin Sonata (K526), as well as the famous *Eine kleine Nachtmusik* (K525). Symphonies by Mozart were performed at concerts in March, and in April, the seventeen-year-old Beethoven came to Vienna with the intention of taking lessons from him, though the brilliant youth was recalled almost as soon as he arrived by news of his mother's illness. Mozart no longer gave big public concerts, partly no doubt because he had lost his novelty value for the Viennese, but also because he preferred to give his time to composition. In this role he was respected but often criticized because, as a Hamburg music critic put it, 'he aims too high in his artful and truly beautiful compositions'. The same writer went on to make specific mention of the quartets dedicated to Haydn which he described as 'too highly sea-soned'. Mozart's income declined as the time he spent com-posing increased, and although he had made a good deal of money in Prague, Wolfgang decided to move at the end of April from central Vienna to the then suburban Landstrasse where he had a considerably lower rent to pay.

There was at this time the additional problem that Mozart's health was poor, and he was further depressed by news of his father's illness. Now sixty-eight years of age, Leopold reported in a letter 'a great change in the condition of my old body'. While expressing the fervent hope that his father's condition would improve, Wolfgang replied with self-revealing thoughts on the subject of death. 'I have for many years', he wrote, 'made myself so familiar with this best friend of man that his image not only holds no terrors for me but also brings me comfort and fortitude. . . . I never go to sleep without re-membering, young as I am' (he was thirty-one) 'that I may never see the following day. Yet nobody who knows me can call me melancholy or dejected in society.' This statement was borne out by acquaintances such as the singer Michael Kelly, who appeared in the original production of *Figaro*, and was a frequent guest of the composer. Mozart always received him kindly, and enjoyed beating him at billiards on 'the ex-cellent billiard table in his house' – an amenity Mozart re-tained to the end. Kelly recalled in his reminiscences that

Mozart was 'remarkably fond of punch, of which beverage I have seen him take copious draughts', but he also confirms that 'this remarkably small man, very thin and pale, with a profusion of fine fair hair of which he was rather vain' was essentially kind-hearted and 'always ready to oblige'.

At the end of May, Mozart had to endure the grief occasioned by news of his father's death. Fortunately there was an abundance of work to distract him, and on 1 October he left Vienna with Constanze for Prague to supervise the staging of *Don Giovanni*. The première had been planned for 14 October to celebrate the marriage of the Emperor's niece, the Archduchess Maria Theresa, but the opera was not ready and *Figaro* was revived instead under Mozart's direction. Rehearsals for the new piece proved difficult and various anecdotes about the final stages of preparation have survived, all more or less apocryphal. It is said that Caterina Bondini, as Zerlina, could not be persuaded to utter a sufficiently agonized shriek from offstage until Mozart crept up behind her and grabbed her so suddenly that she gave vent at once to the required cry; and Mozart is supposed to have written the overture during the dress rehearsal, though in fact it is more likely he wrote it out in the small hours a couple of days before the performance, kept awake with punch and gossip by Constanze.

The first performance when it came on 29 October was a great triumph, in spite of Mozart's anxieties. 'When Herr Mozart entered the orchestra', said a newspaper report, 'he was received with threefold cheers, which again happened when he left it. The opera is extremely difficult to perform but was given, in spite of this, after a short period of study. Everybody on the stage and in the orchestra strained every nerve to thank Mozart by rewarding him with a good performance.' Apart from receiving the usual fee of 50 ducats,

Part of Don Giovanni's serenade 'Deh vieni', with mandolin accompaniment

the composer was also rewarded by the proceeds from the opera's fourth performance, given for his benefit.

Mozart arrived back in Vienna on 12 November, three days before the death at the age of seventy-three of Gluck, news which revived Mozart's hopes of a court appointment. As *Kammermusicus* or Imperial and Royal Court composer, Gluck had been required to provide little more than a few dances for court balls in return for an annual salary of 2000 gulden, a sum described by the old man as 'too much for what I have done but too little for what I could do'.

Naturally Mozart hoped for the succession and this time he was not disappointed. Although he was only to receive 800 gulden annually, this was a sum a good deal larger than he received from the production of an opera, and should have provided him with a degree of financial security. The reason why it failed to do so has remained somewhat mysterious, since although Mozart insisted on keeping up appearances, maintained a servant, and was always well dressed, he and Constanze lived, as we have seen, with careful economy.

In May 1788, *Don Giovanni* was given for the first time in Vienna, and the Emperor attended one of the fifteen performances the opera received in the Austrian capital that year. It was not, however, an overwhelming success. The Emperor is said to have remarked to a courtier that it was 'too difficult for the singers', and told da Ponte that 'such music is not for the teeth of my Viennese'. When the comment was repeated to Mozart he is said to have replied: 'Give them time to chew on it!'

This was a difficult and depressing time for Mozart. He was by no means in the best of health and his income was not equal to the expense of living once again (as his way of life no doubt demanded he should) in the Inner City. He conducted a series of concerts organized by Baron van Swieten for which he updated Handel's *Messiah* in a style which no doubt appealed to contemporary taste but now seems inappropriate.

On an altogether different plane, perhaps for a projected season of concerts at the Casino, Mozart wrote over a period of six weeks that summer his three last symphonies, in E flat K543, G minor K550 and C major K551. He used clarinets instead of oboes in the Symphony No. 39 and the work reflects the warm emotion often associated by the composer with the key of E flat; No. 40 in the 'passionate' key of G minor has an urgent opening theme which sets the tone of an intense yet always graceful composition, and the majestic grandeur of the final symphony in C major, subsequently nicknamed the 'Jupiter', culminates in a brilliant fugal finale. Ironically, at the same time as he was producing these works

of incomparable creative genius, Mozart was forced to post-
pone the publication of recent chamber music for lack of
subscribers, and in June he wrote the first of a long series of
begging letters to his fellow Mason, Michael Puchberg.
Puchberg responded at first with relatively small loans and
was then asked for a much larger sum to be repaid over a
longer period. Early in 1789 Mozart asked for the loan of
100 gulden from the lawyer and magistrate Franz Hofdemel,
then near the end of his Masonic novitiate, but was able to
repay it as promised within four months – perhaps because
of the assistance forthcoming from another member of
Mozart's lodge, Prince Karl Lichnowsky.

In April 1789, the Prince invited the musician to join him on
a business trip to Berlin, where there was much to be hoped
from the patronage of Friedrich Wilhelm II of Prussia, an able
cellist and enlightened lover of music. There were stops on
the way in Prague, where Mozart wrote home to tell Constanze
how much he missed her, and in Dresden, where there were
competitions on the organ and piano between Mozart and
Dresden's leading keyboard player J. W. Hässler, whose
abilities did not impress Wolfgang. In Leipzig, Mozart played
on Bach's organ in St Thomas' Church to a large congregation,
and gave a concert received with enthusiasm by a regrettably
small audience.

The prices charged on this occasion may have been higher
than was customary in Leipzig, but the fact is that Mozart,
for all his reputation as a keyboard performer, was not
universally recognized then as the genius we know him to be
today. While *Figaro* was acclaimed in Hanover that year as
'great and beautiful, full of art, fire and genius', a critic in
Frankfurt at much the same period declared that the music of
Don Giovanni was 'not popular enough to arouse general
interest'. A Copenhagen musical periodical stated that for all

his 'elevated ideas', Mozart did not find ready acceptance because he had 'a decided leaning towards the difficult and unusual'.

Among those who did appreciate Mozart's greatness was Ludwig Tieck, whose memoirs were published in Leipzig in 1855. He reported that in Mozart's lifetime the operas of Dittersdorf were more favourably received in Berlin than those of his rival, though *The Seraglio* was revived there as a gesture of welcome to Mozart when he arrived in the Prussian capital in the Spring of 1789. The story goes that, when Tieck entered the theatre well before the performance was due to start, he met 'a small, unprepossessing figure in a grey overcoat' going from one music desk to another in the orchestra pit, looking carefully through the music. Tieck entered into conversation with the stranger about the theatre, opera and public taste and expressed his admiration of Mozart's operas above all. 'So you often hear Mozart's operas and are fond of them?' the stranger asked. 'That is very good of you, young man.' Soon the stranger was called away by someone on stage, and Tieck enquired the name of the person to whom he had been speaking. He was greatly moved when told it was Mozart himself.

Mozart performed before the King and Queen of Prussia in mid-May and was well rewarded, though he warned his wife not to expect him to bring any great profit back home. So indeed it proved, and although he returned to Vienna in June 1789 with the intention of writing six string quartets and six sonatas for the Prussian King, who had proved himself a prompt and generous client, Mozart was to complete only three of the quartets (with their cello parts designed to suit the talents of the King himself) and one of the sonatas. Very soon the appeals to Puchberg were renewed, for now Constanze, pregnant again, fell seriously ill with a foot complaint.

Mozart, too, was unwell and unable to work. Anxiety no doubt inhibited his efforts at composition and there was no demand in Vienna any longer for his performing talents. 'Good God,' wrote Mozart to his friend in desperation, 'I am coming to you not with thanks but with fresh entreaties. Instead of paying my debts, I am asking for more money. If you really know me, you must sympathize with my anguish at having to do so'. When Puchberg did not immediately comply with the request for another 500 gulden, Mozart wrote again in mid-July, reinforcing his plea with the news that Constanze would have to take a cure at Baden, a spa some 17 miles south of Vienna.

Constanze departed for the spa in August and Mozart visited her there: when he was not with his wife, he seems to have been in a permanent state of jealousy, and was always warning her in letters not to behave in a way likely to jeopardize their reputation. Not that there can have been any great justification for anxiety on this score; Constanze, apart from being ill, was well advanced in pregnancy, giving birth in November to a baby girl who died an hour later of cramp.

More encouraging for the composer was a highly successful revival of *Figaro* in Vienna that summer and a commission from the Emperor for a new Italian opera, to be written once again in collaboration with Lorenzo da Ponte. *Così fan tutte* (All Women Behave Like That) was to occupy Mozart almost to the exclusion of all other compositions until the end of 1789. The one notable exception was the beautiful Clarinet Quintet he wrote for the clarinettist Anton Stadler, who gave the first performance at a concert in the Burgtheater that December.

Da Ponte borrowed some of the ideas for *Così fan tutte* (subtitled *The School for Lovers*) from *La grotta di Trofonio*, an opera produced in 1785 by Antonio Salieri, often regarded as Mozart's arch-rival; it was he and not Mozart who was appointed in 1788 as Kapellmeister, the chief musical officer in the Imperial household.

The story of the opera is beautifully constructed, an elegant and sometimes hilarious comedy which provided Mozart with a great range of expressive possibilities. Two young army officers, Ferrando and Guglielmo, take on a wager with the cynical Don Alfonso that their two girl-friends, Fiordiligi and Dorabella, will remain faithful in their absence. Off they go on active service, leaving their loved ones in tears. As a test of fidelity the young men return not long afterwards disguised as Albanians, and find that, after a little, the girls are ready to forget their promises to Ferrando and Guglielmo. At first shocked and angry, they eventually calm down under the influence of Don Alfonso, who instigated the whole affair, and all ends happily.

We know very little about the genesis of *Così*. Haydn and the long-suffering Puchberg attended a short rehearsal at Mozart's house on New Year's Eve and the opera was first performed with great success at the Burgtheater on 26 January 1790. It has remained among Mozart's best-loved operas ever since, although during the nineteenth century it was sometimes branded as immoral.

Less than a month after the première, the Emperor Joseph II died, and with his departure the partnership of Mozart and da Ponte came to an end. Joseph had championed both poet and musician against the tales spread by their enemies – Mozart claimed that Salieri never ceased to intrigue against him – and after the Emperor's death, da Ponte found it necessary to leave Vienna in a hurry. He fled to Trieste and ultimately found his way to New York, where he died in 1838 at the age of 89, his immortality guaranteed by a trio of operatic masterpieces to which he had made an indispensable contribution.

Chapter Seven

The End and the Beginning

The new Emperor, Leopold II, soon made changes in his musical establishment, but any hopes Mozart might have had of succeeding Salieri as Kapellmeister were quickly dashed. He therefore applied for the post of second Kapellmeister, stressing his ability as a church composer, and continued to beg Puchberg for more money, this time on the grounds that if his poverty became known, it would damage his chances at court 'because unfortunately they do not judge by circumstances but solely by appearances'.

Nothing came of Mozart's attempts to secure a new court appointment, though he retained his position as court composer with a salary that came nowhere near keeping him and his family in the style he thought appropriate. Puchberg received a constant stream of begging letters in the Summer of 1790, in which Mozart declared that financial worry was preventing him from finishing his quartets for the King of Prussia, reiterated the expense of his wife's persistent ill-health (which may have been caused by her constant pregnancies) and complained that he himself often felt too unwell to work, after nights rendered sleepless by pain. One medical theory suggests that Mozart may have been suffering from progressive kidney disease, whose symptoms include the 'pallid skin and bulging eyes' noticed in Mozart's appearance at this time.

Puchberg certainly gave assistance, for Constanze went to Baden again at midsummer, accompanied by her husband 'for economy's sake'; back in Vienna he had begun once again to take pupils as a way of making ends meet, including Franz Xaver Süssmayr, who was to gain a place for himself in musical history by completing Mozart's unfinished Requiem Mass. There was a bitter disappointment in September 1790 when the King and Queen of Naples visited Vienna for the double wedding of their daughters to the Archdukes Franz and Ferdinand; operas were commissioned from Salieri and Josef Weigl and a gala concert was organized, but Mozart was not invited to write anything or to perform.

In a state that must have been near desperation, he decided to follow the court to Frankfurt for the coronation there of the new Emperor on 9 October; he felt sure that the festivities would provide him with some opportunity. Pawning his silver to hire a carriage, he set off in a sudden revival of high spirits and told Constanze from Frankfurt that he was being invited everywhere, though every morning he stayed in his 'hole of a bedroom' to compose. A week after the coronation, Mozart gave a concert in the municipal playhouse which included the D major Concerto K537, consequently known as the 'Coronation'. One of those present, Count Ludwig von Bentheim-Steinfurt, remarked in his travel diary that 'there were not many people'.

Later in October there were visits to Mainz, where Mozart was paid rather more generously for a concert than he admitted to Constanze, and to Mannheim where the cast of the first production of *Figaro* in the city begged him to help with rehearsals. Finally on his way home to Vienna he paused in Munich, where the Elector invited him to play at a concert in honour of the King of Naples. Recalling his earlier humiliation, Mozart wrote bitterly to his wife: 'it is *greatly* to the credit of the Viennese court that the king has to hear me in a foreign country!'

An invitation awaited Wolfgang on his return home which must have been attractive. The London impresario Robert May O'Reilly had written offering Mozart £300 if he would come to England for six months and write two operas. At much the same time, Mozart was introduced in Vienna to Johann Peter Salomon, who also invited him to visit London. Haydn, as we know, accepted Salomon's invitation, though he was old enough to be Mozart's father, and Mozart considered he was unwise to travel so far when nearly sixty. The younger man was not willing to go to England, partly because he was already committed in Vienna and no doubt also because he was reluctant to leave his wife and friends yet again. Mozart is said to have waved farewell to the departing Haydn with tears in his eyes, and the prophetic words 'I fear we shall never see each other again.'

Da Ponte recalled in his memoirs how he too had tried to persuade Mozart to join him in London, and quoted a letter from the composer in which Mozart speaks of the imminent approach of death and of his imperative need to work while he is still able to do so. The letter may not be authentic, but there is no doubt of the extreme pressure under which he forced himself to labour during his last year. Sometime in 1790 he had received from the actor and impresario Emanuel Schikaneder, a fellow-Mason, the outline and part of the text of what was to become *The Magic Flute*; some parts of the score, including the humorous duet between Papageno and Papagena, were delivered by the Spring of 1791. Schikaneder also wrote the words for a Masonic cantata Mozart had to complete for the opening of a new lodge in November that year. In March, Mozart performed his serene last piano concerto, K595 in B flat; he produced two great string quintets

in D and E flat, K593 and K614; a commission arrived in July
1791 from the theatre in Prague for a new opera for the
coronation in the Bohemian capital in September of the
Emperor Leopold; and during the summer, a mysterious
stranger came to the composer with a commission for a
Requiem Mass, a circumstance regarded by Mozart as a
premonition of his own death. In fact the mystery arose from
a secret plan on the part of Count Franz Walsegg-Stuppach,
who wished to have the Requiem performed as a tribute of
his own composition to the memory of his dead wife.

If Mozart's death was not actually hastened by overwork,
as many believed, the pace of his activity in 1791 can have
done nothing to improve his condition. We read of nights when
he did not get to bed till 2 am and rose again to begin work
for the day at 4. Preparation of *The Magic Flute* brought
him into contact with Schikaneder's theatrical company and
he would often spend long social evenings with them, especially when his wife was absent, as she was again during the
summer months of 1791, taking the waters at Baden. What
hostile observers were quick to call loose living was explained
by Mozart as part of his imperative need for congenial company. 'It is not at all good for me to be alone when I have
something on my mind', he explained to his wife in the course
of describing how he spent one evening when she was away.
'I went to the Kasperle Theatre to see the new opera, then,
when passing the coffee house, I looked in to see if Loibl was
there, but there was not a sign of him. I again took a meal at
the "Krone" simply in order not to be alone, and there at least
I found someone to talk to. Then I went straight to bed. . . .'
Another letter is even more revealing of the composer's state
of mind in the summer of 1791: 'I can't describe what I have
been feeling, a kind of emptiness which hurts me dreadfully –
a kind of longing which is never satisfied, which never ceases

Title-page of the first edition of the Magic Flute *libretto with (left)*
frontispiece showing Egyptian motifs and Masonic symbols, and (right)
costume design for Papageno

and which persists, nay rather increases daily . . . if I go to the
piano and sing something out of my new opera, I have to
stop at once, for this stirs my emotions too deeply.' When
Constanze returned to Vienna, bearing a sixth child on 26
July, one hopes that at least some of her husband's private
misery was assuaged.

In the second half of August, the Mozarts set out for Prague
for the production of *La clemenza di Tito*, the opera Mozart
composed for the Emperor's coronation in that part of his
dominions. The story, adapted from Metastasio, tells of the

Roman Emperor Titus. It shows monarchy in a very favour-able light, as might be expected on such an occasion. In any case Mozart was doubtless still hoping to soften Leopold's hard-hearted indifference, and his Titus displays truly amazing clemency even to those who plot against his life and set fire to Rome itself.

The music, some of which was written in the carriage on the way to Prague with the assistance of Süssmayr, by now a devoted amanuensis, is generally not on the same level as the great works of Mozart's last period, but there is a splendid finale to the first act, and two of the arias have the added interest of obbligato parts for clarinet and basset horn which were performed by Anton Stadler. On his return to Vienna, Mozart found time to compose for Stadler a Clarinet Con-certo whose autumnal beauties match those of the marvellous Clarinet Quintet.

Soon after his arrival in Prague, Mozart attended and may have conducted a festival performance of *Don Giovanni* and four days later, on 6 September, *La clemenza di Tito* was given before an audience which included the Emperor; after arriving an hour late, he accorded the piece a polite reception. There was little of the glamorous socializing which had attended the success of *Figaro*, and according to one account, by the time Mozart left Prague after this visit, he was obviously ill and taking medicine continually; though he was still cap-able of displaying a kind of 'gay seriousness'.

Back in Vienna, he was plunged into the final preparations for *The Magic Flute* (*Die Zauberflöte*), which was first per-formed at the Theater auf der Wieden on 30 September, with Mozart directing from the keyboard. It was a success from the start: no less than twenty performances were given in October and Mozart had the gratification of seeing audiences grow in size as the run went on.

50   *Those who know Vienna today will recognize this romanticized image of Mozart, but may think the background inappropriate. The statue was originally erected in the Albrechtsplatz behind the State Opera in 1896, and was subsequently moved to its present position in the Burggarten. >*

51–53 The Magic Flute, *with its elusive fairy-tale quality, has always offered an attractive challenge to operatic producers and designers.* Above: Tamino, the Three Ladies and Papageno *in a scene from Act I of the opera. Stage setting designed by Nesslthaler and painted by Joseph Gayl, possibly for the first performance in 1791.* Opposite, above: *the Queen of the Night scene designed by Karl Friedrich Schinkel for a Berlin production of* The Magic Flute, *1816.* Opposite, below: *David Hockney's design for Act II scene 1 of the opera as staged at Glyndebourne in 1978.*

55 (K623). *Dr Ludwig Ritter von Köchel (1800–1877), the Austrian geologist and botanist who devised the first comprehensive catalogue of Mozart's works – hence the familiar 'K' numbers. The catalogue has been revised and updated but Köchel's numbering is still widely used.*

56–59 Opposite, above: *Baden, the fashionable spa near Vienna, drawn by Lorenz Janscha. Constanze sought a cure for persistent ill-health by taking the waters here, and Mozart wrote his well-known motet* Ave Verum Corpus *for the Baden choirmaster. Opposite, below left: Constanze, who died in 1842, surviving her husband by more than fifty years. She continued to champion Mozart's cause. Oil portrait by Hans Hansen, 1802, Opposite, below right: Mozart's two surviving children, Franz Xaver (left) and Karl Thomas. Franz became a musician; Karl was able to buy an estate in Italy with profits from* The Marriage of Figaro. *Above: the house in Vienna where Mozart died. He and Constanze had taken up residence on the first floor in 1790.*

60, 61 *The death mask, previously thought to be spurious, is now accepted by some scholars as authentic. The last notes Mozart committed to paper belong to the Lacrimosa of the Requiem Mass, later completed by Süssmayr.*

The Magic Flute is a strange mixture of solemn ceremony based on Masonic rituals and light-hearted comedy bordering on farce. The story arises from the eternal enmity between good and evil, personified in the characters of Sarastro the High Priest and the Queen of the Night. The Queen's daughter, Pamina, is held by Sarastro, and the young Tamino sets out to rescue her, believing, under the Queen's influence, that Sarastro is the evil one. Tamino is aided in his quest by a magic flute and by a bird-catcher, Papageno, who is equipped with a magic glockenspiel. Tamino soon discovers that he has been deceived about the nature of Sarastro and, having fallen in love with Pamina, is initiated into the priestly brotherhood. Both the lovers are subjected to ceremonial ordeals, and the Queen of the Night makes a final attempt to rescue Pamina, but the power of goodness triumphs and all ends happily.

The score is rich in great music throughout, but Sarastro's two bass arias and the coloratura displays of the Queen of the Night have become lasting favourites, together with Tamino's lovely tenor aria expressing his love for Pamina when he is shown her portrait, and Papageno's aria on his first entrance when he describes his profession as a bird-catcher.

Papageno was played in the first production by Emanuel Schikaneder himself, an accomplished and popular comedian, and Mozart enjoyed teasing him when the chance arose. Writing to Constanze, who again spent some time in Baden during October, Mozart related how, on one occasion, he decided to take over the offstage glockenspiel which was sounded as Schikaneder mimed the action on stage. 'Just for fun', wrote Mozart, 'at the point when Schikaneder has a pause, I played an arpeggio. He was startled, looked behind the wings and saw me. When he had his next pause, I played no arpeggio. This time he stopped and refused to go on. I guessed what he was thinking and played another chord.

Then he struck the glockenspiel and told it to shut up! Everybody laughed because they realized for the first time that Schikaneder was not playing the glockenspiel himself.'

On 13 October, Mozart had the gratification of taking Salieri to a performance and witnessing his wholehearted approval of the work: 'he listened and watched most attentively, and from the overture to the last chorus there was not a single number that did not call forth from him a "bravo" or a "bello"!'

It is good to know that *The Magic Flute* brought a real measure of satisfaction to Mozart, though one report in a Berlin musical journal said that in spite of the cost of the production and the magnificence of the scenery, it 'failed to have the hoped-for success', the writer adding that Vienna was still impatiently awaiting an operatic renaissance when Cimarosa arrived to replace Salieri as Imperial Kapellmeister. The same periodical, however, displayed greater perception in its critique of a Berlin production of *Don Giovanni* on 10 October 1791; it read: 'We must unite profound knowledge of the art with the happiest talent for inventing lovely melodies, and then link both with the greatest possible originality in order to obtain the most faithful picture of Mozart's musical genius.' Evidently there were some discerning individuals who valued Mozart at his true worth even during his short lifetime.

Constanze returned from Baden in mid-October, and while walking with her in the Prater one day, Mozart burst into tears, saying that he thought he had been poisoned and would not live long. Josef Deiner, landlord of a Viennese tavern, *The Silver Snake*, found him similarly depressed one day in November, 'looking unusually pale, his powdered fair hair in disarray and little pigtail carelessly tied'. Mozart had ordered wine instead of his customary beer, but left it untouched. 'You look quite ill and wretched, Maestro', said Deiner. 'I heard you were in Prague and the Bohemian air has not done you any good. But you'll be alright!' 'No,' replied Mozart, 'I fear there won't be much more music making. I've got a chill coming on that I can't account for. You drink my wine. I'll have a fire lighted this very day.'

The composer recovered sufficiently to direct his new cantata (K623) at the dedication of a Masonic temple on 18 November but two days later took to his bed with swelling of the hands and feet, a sort of paralysis and fits of vomiting. During the next few days, between visits from his doctors, Mozart continued to work feverishly on his Requiem, explaining his ideas to Süssmayr and working out some details on the pianoforte in his room; there were even short rehearsals of parts of the work round his sick bed, including one on 4 December in which he sang the alto part: during the Lacrimosa he was unable to continue for weeping. Someone sang the bird-catcher's song from *The Magic Flute* to try and cheer him up, but Mozart knew that death was not far off. Constanze's sister Sophie went for a priest, and Dr Closset was called that evening from the theatre, but he could do nothing. Mozart died at five minutes to one on the morning of 5 December 1791, at the age of 35. There has been much subsequent controversy as to the cause of his death. Some authorities believe that he died of a form of rheumatic fever; others who support the theory that Mozart was suffering from progressive kidney failure believe that he died following the onset of an uraemic coma.

In her husband's album, Constanze wrote soon after his death: 'Dearly beloved husband; Mozart—never to be forgotten by me or by the whole of Europe—now thou too art at peace—eternal peace! ! . . . About one o'clock in the morning of the 5th of December in this year he left in his 36th year—alas! all too soon!—this good—but ungrateful world!—dear

God!—For 8 years we were joined together by the most tender bond, never to be broken here below!—O! could I soon be joined with thee for ever. Thy grievously afflicted wife Constanze Mozart *née* Weber'

Constanze was to survive her husband by fifty years. She died in 1842 after marrying a man she first met in 1797, Georg Nikolaus Nissen. In the years immediately following Wolfgang's death she devoted herself to organizing concerts of his works, touring widely in Germany and Bohemia without apparently showing any sign of the ill health which had pursued her during Mozart's last years.

Together with the tributes which appeared in the musical press, rumours began to spread regarding the manner of Mozart's death. Because his body swelled up after he died the idea gained ground that he had been poisoned, and Salieri's name was linked with the crime. This story became widely current again in the mid-1820s when Salieri, who had become mentally deranged, claimed in his ravings that he had done away with Mozart by poisoning him, and the suggestion has never been conclusively disproved. It does, however, seem extremely unlikely, and the Viennese physician Dr Eduard Guldener gains our sympathy with his public declaration of Salieri's innocence in 1824: 'I shall have the greatest pleasure', he wrote, 'if this can contribute to giving the lie to the horrible calumny on the excellent Salieri.'

Mozart's burial is another subject of controversy. It has often been said that he was given a pauper's funeral, but the evidence suggests that although it was very modest, it was not out of keeping with the fashion of the time. Very simple funeral arrangements were often made, in accordance with the express wishes of the late Emperor Joseph II. There was a short service in a side-chapel in St Stephen's Cathedral attended by a few fellow-Masons; others present included

Baron van Swieten, who was quick to come to Constanze's aid, and Salieri. The fact that none of them followed the body to the cemetery of St Marx, where it was buried in a common grave, again seems to have been in accordance with the custom of the time among enlightened people.

A tablet now marks the spot in St Stephen's Cathedral where the funeral service was held, but Constanze had no memorial erected to her husband, feeling confident that posterity would see to that. She and her two surviving children, Karl and Franz Xaver, the last to be born, were soon receiving financial assistance from a number of sources. There were benefit concerts, Beethoven played a Mozart concerto during a Vienna production of *La Clemenza di Tito*, Friedrich Wilhelm of Prussia paid a good price for some manuscripts and the Emperor Leopold provided a pension. Franz Xaver became a modestly successful musician, Karl a well-respected landowner in Italy, his estate purchased with receipts from performances of *Figaro* in Paris.

As for their father, nearly two hundred years after his death, we are still unable to do justice in words to the greatness of his genius. Amazing in all the many kinds of music he essayed, he was the creator of the piano concerto as we know it, superb in symphonic and chamber music, produced magnificent choral works for the church, and was arguably the greatest of all opera composers. For a time the true stature of Mozart as a composer was obscured, partly by the reputation for personal irresponsibility he left behind him. Two years after his death, an almanac of deaths for the year 1791 carried this unsympathetic paragraph about Mozart: 'In Vienna he married Constanze Weber and found her a good mother of two children of their union and a worthy wife, who moreover sought to restrain him from many foolishnesses and excesses. Despite a considerable income, he yet, in consequence of his exceptional sensuality and domestic disorder, left his family nothing beyond the glory of his name and the attention of a large public fixed upon them.' A diarist of the period noted the zest with which Mozart carried on his battle with Salieri and his other rivals, and alleged that he played billiards for high stakes all night long – 'he was very thoughtless, but his wife excused him'.

Karoline Pichler, writing her memoirs in the 1840s, recalled how she knew both Mozart and Haydn. 'They were men', she wrote, 'in whose personal intercourse there was absolutely no other sign of unusual power of intellect and almost no trace of intellectual culture, nor of any scholarly or other higher interests. A rather ordinary turn of mind, silly jokes and in the case of the former, an irresponsible way of life, were all that distinguished them in society.'

Looking back on Mozart's life, we can appreciate the perceptive insight of Mozart's sister Nannerl when she said quite simply that Mozart remained a child all his years. The practical matters which occupy and satisfy so many adults had no meaning for him. He was truly alive only when creating music in the solitude of his room, so his real existence remained hidden – as da Ponte put it, writing in New York in 1830 – 'like a precious stone buried in the bowels of the earth'.

Only when Mozart himself was buried did the world begin to learn what an abundance of life he had bequeathed to us.

Chronology

1756 Born at Salzburg, 27 January

1761 Composes his first pieces, an Andante and Allegro for solo keyboard

1762 Plays before the Elector of Bavaria. In September to Vienna, where Mozart and his sister Nannerl appear twice before the Empress Maria Theresa

1763 Beginning of the Grand Tour. Concerts in, among other places, Munich, Augsburg, Mainz and Frankfurt, on the way to Paris, where they remain for five months. Mozart's first music appears in print: two pairs of keyboard sonatas

1764 Arrive in England and stay for fifteen months, meeting J. C. Bach

1765 Concerts in the Netherlands, where both children become seriously ill

1766 Back in Salzburg, Mozart arranges some concertos from sonatas by various composers and writes the Latin intermezzo *Apollo et Hyacinthus* for the university graduation ceremony

1767 To Vienna. Wolfgang and Nannerl both contract smallpox

1768 *La finta semplice* composed for Vienna but not in the event given there. A one-act Singspiel,

Bastien und Bastienne, commissioned by Dr Franz Anton Mesmer, the inventor of 'magnetism therapy'

1769 Made third Konzertmeister to the Salzburg Court Chapel

1770 Leopold and Wolfgang in Italy; Count Firmian their chief patron in Milan. Mozart writes his first string quartet. Meets the composer Padre Martini and the famous castrato Farinelli. After hearing the Allegri *Miserere* in the Sistine Chapel, Mozart writes it out from memory. In Rome he is made a Knight of the Golden Spur. *Mitridate* a great success in Milan.

1771 A second Italian visit sees the first performance of a serenata, *Ascanio in Alba*

1772 Writes a dramatic serenata, *Il sogno di Scipione*, for the installation ceremony of the new Prince-Archbishop, Count Colloredo, and begins to receive an income of 150 florins as Konzertmeister, but Leopold and Wolfgang restless in Salzburg. Third Italian tour; *Lucio Silla* performed in Milan

1773 Writes quartets K168–173 in Vienna. Several symphonies (the Salzburg symphonies) this year and the following, notably K183 in G minor and K201 in A major

1775 Premières of *La finta giardiniera* and *Il rè pastore*. Composition of five violin concertos

1776 Several piano concertos. *Serenata notturna*. Haffner Serenade. Masses for the Court Chapel

1777 Dissatisfaction with Colloredo erupts. Mozart leaves his service and begins tour with his mother, visiting Mannheim, where he fails to secure a court post but composes some flute quartets and concertos and falls in love with a singer, Aloysia Weber

1778 Paris tour; his mother dies. 'Paris' Symphony. Leopold urges Wolfgang to return to Salzburg; reluctantly he does. No major posts or commissions offered

1779 Obtains expected post as Court Organist at Salzburg. Symphonies K318 and 319. Sinfonia Concertante for violin and viola K364. Coronation Mass

1780 Writes *Idomeneo* for Munich. Aloysia Weber marries the court actor Joseph Lange, who subsequently executed a famous (unfinished) portrait of Mozart

1781 Archbishop summons Mozart to Vienna for accession of Emperor Joseph II. Mozart finally leaves Colloredo's service and hopes for a better future in Vienna, where he also becomes increasingly intimate with Aloysia's sister Constanze. Competition with Clementi

1782 The *Abduction from the Seraglio*. Haffner Symphony. Marries Constanze

1783 Their first child, Raimund Leopold, born. After several delays, they travel to Salzburg for Leopold to meet Constanze; they stay about three months during which time the baby dies. Returning via Linz, Mozart composes K425, the 'Linz' Symphony, 'at breakneck speed'

1784 Begins catalogue of his works. Becomes a Freemason. Six piano concertos

1785 Reputation as a composer and pianist reaches its peak. Three new piano concertos. Publication of six string quartets dedicated to Haydn; receives accolade from Haydn

1786 *The Impresario* performed in the Orangery in Schönbrunn Palace. Première of *The Marriage of Figaro*. Piano concertos in A (K488), C minor (K491) and C major (K503)

1787 'Prague' Symphony (K504) given on a visit there. After several months back in Vienna, returns to Prague for first production of *Don Giovanni*. String quintets in C major and G minor. Succeeds Gluck as court *Kammermusicus*

1788 Letters to Michael Puchberg, a fellow-Mason, pleading for loans. The three last symphonies

1789 Journeying via Prague, Dresden and Leipzig (where he improvises on Bach's organ) he visits Potsdam and Berlin, agreeing to write some quartets for King Friedrich Wilhelm II (K575, 589 and 590). Clarinet Quintet for Anton Stadler

1790 Première of *Così fan tutte*. Travels unofficially to Frankfurt

to attend coronation festivities of new emperor, Leopold II

1791 Unsuccessful petition for post of Kapellmeister at St Stephen's Cathedral. Mysterious commission of Requiem Mass. *La clemenza di Tito* and *The Magic Flute*. Clarinet Concerto for Stadler. Death in Vienna, 5 December

Further Reading

ANDERSON, EMILY (ed.) *Letters of Mozart and his Family*, London 1938; rev. edn ed. A Hyatt King and M. Carolan, London and New York 1966

BBC MUSIC GUIDES: *Mozart Chamber Music* (A. Hyatt King), London 1968; *Mozart Piano Concertos* (Philip Radcliffe), London 1978; *Mozart Wind and String Concertos* (A. Hyatt King), London 1978

BLOM, ERIC *Mozart*, New York 1949; rev. edn London 1974

BROPHY, BRIGID *Mozart the Dramatist*, London and New York 1964

DENT, EDWARD J. *Mozart's Operas*, London and New York 1955 (3rd edn)

DEUTSCH, OTTO ERICH *Mozart: A Documentary Biography*, London 1965; Stanford, Calif. 1966

— *Mozart and his World in Contemporary Pictures*, London and New York 1961

HUTCHINGS, ARTHUR *A Companion to Mozart's Piano Concertos*, London and New York 1950 (2nd edn)

— *Mozart: the Man, the Musician*, London and New York 1976

KEYS, IVOR *Mozart: his Music in his Life*, London 1980

LANDON, H. C. ROBBINS *Haydn: A Documentary Study*, London and New York 1981

— and MITCHELL, DONALD (eds) *The Mozart Companion*, London 1965 (2nd edn); New York 1970

LEVEY, MICHAEL *The Life and Death of Mozart*, London and New York 1971

MANN, WILLIAM *The Operas of Mozart*, New York 1976; London 1977

OSBORNE, CHARLES *The Complete Operas of Mozart*, London and New York 1978

OTTAWAY, HUGH *Mozart*, London 1979; Detroit 1980

RAYNOR, HENRY *Mozart*, London 1978

SADIE, STANLEY *Mozart*, London 1966; New York 1970

SCHENK, ERICH *Mozart and his Times*, New York 1959; London 1960

List of Illustrations

Franz Xaver Jungwierth after Bernardo Bellotto (1720–1780). Staatliche Graphische Sammlung, Munich
21 Hieronymus Colloredo, Prince-Archbishop of Salzburg. Detail from oil portrait by Franz Xaver König, 1772. Abbey of St Peter, Salzburg
22 Aloysia Weber as Zémire in Grétry's opera Zémire et Azor. Detail from engraving by Johannes Esaias Nilson, 1784. Internationale Stiftung Mozarteum, Salzburg
23 Paris. View from the old grain market towards Pont Notre-Dame, 1782
24 Redoutensaal, Vienna. Engraving by M. Weinmann, 1748. Österreichische Nationalbibliothek, Vienna
25 Baron Grimm. Wash drawing by Louis Carrogis de Carmontelle, 1758. Musée Condé, Chantilly. Photo Giraudon
26 Posthumous oil portrait of Mozart by Barbara Krafft, painted Salzburg 1819 for Joseph Sonnleithner's Gallery of Composers. Gesellschaft der Musikfreunde, Vienna
27 Marriage contract, dated 3 August 1782. On loan to the British Library, London, from the heirs of Stefan Zweig
28 Constanze Mozart. Oil painting by Joseph Lange. Hunterian Museum and Art Gallery, University of Glasgow
29 Vienna, by Bernardo Bellotto, 1759–60. Kunsthistorisches Museum, Vienna
30 Antonio Salieri (1750–1825). Lithograph of 1815. Bertarelli Archives, Milan
31 Muzio Clementi (1752–1832). From a painting by Thomas Hardy engraved by the artist. Bertarelli Archives, Milan
32 Christoph Willibald Gluck (1714–1787). Portrait (detail) by J.-S. Duplessis, 1775. Collection Comtesse d'Albufera. Photo Giraudon
33 Haydn at the age of 67. Oil portrait by J. C. Roesler. Painted in Vienna, 1799. Courtesy the Heather Professor of Music, Oxford University. Photo Bodleian Library, Oxford
34 Meeting of a Masonic lodge in Vienna. Anonymous painting, c. 1780. Historisches Museum der Stadt Wien, Vienna
35 Count Thun, surrounded by Masonic symbols. Engraving by Gottlieb Friedrich Riedel, after a painting by A. Rähmel, 1787. Historisches Museum der Stadt Wien, Vienna
36 Unfinished portrait of Mozart at the age of 26 by Joseph Lange. Internationale Stiftung Mozarteum, Salzburg
37 Emperor Joseph II. Detail of painting by Pompeo Batoni, 1769. Kunsthistorisches Museum, Vienna
38 The Lindenallee in the Augarten, Vienna. Drawing and engraving by Johann Ziegler. Albertina, Vienna
39 Vienna, Inner City; view of St Peter's Church and St Stephen's Cathedral. Photo Austrian National Tourist Office, London
40 Frank Finlay as Salieri and Richard O'Callaghan as Mozart in Peter Shaffer's play Amadeus. Photo Zoë Dominic
41 Autograph manuscript of Cherubino's aria 'Non so più' from The Marriage of Figaro. On loan to the

British Library, London, from the heirs of Stefan Zweig

42 Lorenzo da Ponte. Detail from engraving by Michele Pekenino after a painting by Nathaniel Rogers (1788–1844). Österreichische National-bibliothek, Vienna

43 Interior of the Burgtheater, Vienna. Österreichische National-bibliothek, Vienna.

44 The Burgtheater, St Michael's Square, Vienna. Drawing and engraving by Carl Schütz, 1789. Albertina, Vienna

45 Contemporary view of Prague. Watercolour by Karl Postl (1769–1818). Albertina, Vienna

46 Scene from *Don Giovanni*, a film by Joseph Losey. Photo courtesy Artificial Eye.

47 Interior of the Villa Betramka, Prague. Mansell Collection

48 Courtyard with garden, in the main street of the Landstrasse suburb of Vienna. Österreichische National-bibliothek, Vienna

49 Mozart's Walter clavier of 1780. Internationale Stiftung Mozarteum, Salzburg

50 The Mozart statue standing in the Albrechtsplatz, Vienna, where it was erected on 21 April 1896. Now in the Burggarten. Mansell Collection

51 Engraving of the stage setting for Act I of *The Magic Flute* (possibly that for the first performance in 1791). Joseph Gayl was the scene painter and Nesslthaler the designer. Öster-reichische Nationalbibliothek, Vienna

52 Queen of the Night scene. Wash-coloured engraving after a design by Karl Friedrich Schinkel for the per-formance of *The Magic Flute* in Berlin, 1816. Staatsbibliothek, Berlin. Bildarchiv Preussischer Kulturbesitz

53 David Hockney's design, 'A Palm Grove', for Act II Scene 1 of *The Magic Flute*, staged at Glyndebourne in 1978. Photo courtesy Glyndebourne Festival Opera

54 Last page of the catalogue of his own works which Mozart began on 9 February 1784. On loan to the British Library, London, from the heirs of Stefan Zweig

55 Dr Ludwig Ritter von Köchel (1800–1877). Compiler of first com-prehensive Mozart catalogue. Inter-nationale Stiftung Mozarteum, Salzburg

56 Detail of a drawing of Baden. Albertina, Vienna

57 Constanze Mozart. After the oil portrait by Hans Hansen, 1802. Internationale Stiftung Mozarteum, Salzburg

58 Mozart's children, Franz Xaver (left) and Karl Thomas. Oil portrait *c*.1798 by Hans Hansen. Internationale Stiftung Mozarteum, Salzburg

59 The house where Mozart died. After a watercolour by E. Hutter, 1847

60 Mozart's death-mask. BBC Copy-right

61 The Lacrimosa from the Requiem. Österreichische Nationalbibliothek, Vienna

Index

Figures in italics refer to illustrations